What Others Say About the Impact of the First Edition of This Book

"I have read your *No B.S. Time Management for Entrepreneurs* three times since mid-June. Here are the recommendations from your book I've implemented: I've set up a time-blocked schedule for myself; I keep phone time to a minimum, clustered; I link daily work to goals; I've re-arranged certain things, like my weekly commute to a research center, to off-peak times. My income for July topped $20,000.00—not the $10,000.00 I had as my goal. I know that for many of your folks this is merely a sneeze. But for me, it's a gigantic leap. And unheard of for a one-person genealogy business. Thank you seems like such a small acknowledgment for such a gigantic boost in my business productivity."

—ARLENE H. EAKLE, THE GENEALOGICAL INSTITUTE, UTAH

"People often ask me—'Tony, you're a writer, salesman, workshop trainer, leader of multiple organizations, father of three young children, in good physical shape. How do you pull it all off?' My answer: your book! I read it again every six months. The amazing thing is, I spend fewer hours, my income keeps rising. Your advice can make anyone a master of time, not a slave to it."

—TONY RUBLESKI, AUTHOR OF *MIND CAPTURE*; V.P. SALES, CAPTIVE AUDIENCE ADVERTISING, MICHIGAN

"My name is Sam Beckford. I'm 33 years old. My wife Valerie and I started our first dance studio from scratch in 1995, with no money, no investors, no contacts in the teaching business, and debt. We built our business up to three studio locations with over 2800 students in just eight years. Each of our locations makes a profit of over $100,000.00 a year. We are able to run our studios at this level without being slaves to our business. In addition, we host a large seminar twice a year and provide ongoing coaching to other studio owners. For most of the year we work from our home office, only go into the studios three to four hours a week, take great vacations, and things run smoothly without us being there. Dan Kennedy has been a great mentor and example to me, not just for his smart marketing, but also for the way in which he controls his time, business, and life."

—SAM BECKFORD, VANCOUVER, B.C., CANADA

N B.S.

TIME MANAGEMENT
FOR ENTREPRENEURS
SECOND EDITION

**THE ULTIMATE
NO-HOLDS BARRED
KICK BUTT
TAKE NO PRISONERS
GUIDE TO TIME
PRODUCTIVITY & SANITY**

Dan S. Kennedy

Entrepreneur
PRESS®

Publisher: Entrepreneur Press
Cover Design: Andrew Welyczko
Production and Composition: Eliot House Productions

This publication is designed to provide accurate and authoritative information in regard to the subject matter covered. It is sold with the understanding that the publisher is not engaged in rendering legal, accounting, or other professional services. If legal advice or other expert assistance is required, the services of a competent professional person should be sought.

Library of Congress Cataloging-in-Publication Data
Kennedy, Dan S., 1954–
    No B.S. time management for entrepreneurs: the ultimate no holds
  barred, kick butt, take no prisoners guide to time productivity & sanity
  / by Dan S. Kennedy.—Second edition.
    p.   cm.
    Includes index.
  ISBN-10: 1-59918-509-1 (pbk.)
  ISBN-13: 978-1-59918-509-5 (pbk.)
    1. Time management. I. Title.
  HD69.T54K466 2013
  650.1'1—dc23   2013018445

Contents

CHAPTER 13

Reasons Why a Year Passes and No Meaningful Progress Is Made 167

Dan Kennedy's No B.S. Time Truths 175

Index 179

Free Offer 187

What Can You Get
from This Book?

by Bill Gough

C an one book motivate you to radically alter your thinking about a familiar subject, your business practices, your personal behavior, for the better?

In 2004, a peer I respect tremendously encouraged me to take a look at the No B.S. series of books written by Dan Kennedy, and he recommended I start with the book on time management. He said these were '"real world books" that I could trust.

The first chapter of Dan's *No B.S. Time Management for Entrepreneurs* literally changed my life—and it did it almost overnight. The simple exercise in that chapter made me realize the REAL value of my time when I'm performing productive work. This was a huge "Ah-Ha Moment" for me. Of course, we all know our time has to be valuable. That wasn't a new idea for me, and I'm sure it won't be for you either. But the clarity this exercise created for me was new.

Many things changed for me right then, not only in how I managed my time and work, but also the time and work of my employees in our busy, successful, but often stressed insurance agency. We had good people and good processes, but we had a lot of bad management of time. Pushed by this book, I focused on devoting the right shares of time to the most profitable processes and activities, with the right people performing the right tasks, and everything held financially accountable.

I already had a very *successful* career and business. Guided by this book, I created a *better* career and a *stronger* business. Since the early 1990s, and still today, I've been in the top 5% of all Allstate Insurance Agency owners, for a couple reasons. I like to compete and win. Also, I do really well at watching and learning from other exceptionally successful business leaders, like Dan Kennedy. In 2008, in large part thanks to my new and improved time management, I was able to keep my agency at top performance and develop a second company coaching other agency owners. I founded BGIMarketing.com to help other agency owners improve every aspect of their businesses and business lives, and we now provide training for owners, sales agents, and staffs; coaching; and many time-saving marketing tools and programs to thousands of agency owners all over America.

I also began using the strategies in this book in my personal life. Pre-Kennedy, I was *that* Dad at my kids' baseball games—with the phone glued to my ear, conducting business, never really enjoying the moments that never repeat, that you can never get back. The book even helped prepare me for the biggest challenge our family has ever faced, when my son, Bill Gough III, died in a drowning accident at age 23. A percentage of every dollar generated at BGI Marketing goes into the Bill Gough III Memorial Charity Fund, and to date, we have donated over $400,000.00 to charities, with a goal to exceed $1 million by 2018. You can see the whole story and learn more about my business at www.BGIMarketing.com.

I did *not* just read this book, nod at places, and place it on a shelf. I acted on it. I hope you will too.

The Need for Extraordinary
Measures

It gets late early out here.

—Yogi Berra

Wimps and Willy Lomans—beware! This book is not for the faint of heart, fawningly polite, or desperate to be liked.

Hopefully, you have picked up this book because you are an entrepreneur, your time is incredibly valuable to you, and you are constantly "running out of it."

If you know me, then you've also been motivated to get this book to find out how I manage to do all that I do. I have been asked so often, by what seems like everybody who becomes familiar with my life, how the devil I fit it all in, that I sat down and wrote out the answer—this book. If you don't know me, then your curiosity about my methods may be further piqued by the description of my activities that follow this Preface. If you know me, skip that section.

As a very busy, sometimes frantic, time-pressured entrepreneur, awash in opportunity, too often surrounded by nitwits and slower-than-molasses-pouring-uphill folk, I understand your needs, desires, and frustrations. The multiple demands on an entrepreneur's time are *extraordinary*. So I am here to tell you that you need to take extraordinary measures to match those demands. Measures so radical and extreme that others may question your sanity. This is no ordinary time management book for the deskbound or the person doing just one job. This book is expressly for the wearer of many hats, the inventive, opportunistic entrepreneur who can't resist piling more and more responsibility onto his own shoulders, who has many more great ideas than time and resources to take advantage of them, who runs (not walks) through each day. I'm you, and this is our book.

As you have undoubtedly discovered, time is the most precious asset any entrepreneur possesses. Time to solve problems. Time to invent, create, think, and plan. Time to gather and assimilate information. Time to develop sales, marketing, management, and profit breakthroughs. Time to network. Probably not a day goes by that you don't shove something aside, sigh, and say to yourself: *"If I could only find an extra hour* to work on this, it'd make a huge difference in our business." Well, I'm going to give you that extra hour. But what we're about to do here together is much bigger than just eking out an extra hour here or there. We are going to drastically re-engineer your entire relationship with time.

I've had more than 35 years of high-pressure, high-wire-without-a-net entrepreneurial activity—starting, buying, developing, selling, succeeding in and failing in businesses, going broke, getting profoundly rich, and helping clients in hundreds of different fields. Here's what I've come to believe to be the single biggest "secret" of extraordinary personal, financial, and entrepreneurial success combined: the use or misuse (or abuse by others) of your time. The degree to which you achieve peak productivity will determine your success. So this book is about everything that can be done to achieve peak personal productivity.

Just thinking about it is a big step in the right direction. Awareness helps a lot. There's a reason why you can't find a wall clock in a casino to save your life—those folks stealing your money do not want you to be aware of the passing of time. And that tells you something useful right there: You want to be very aware, all the time, of the passing of time. It is to your advantage to be very conscious of the passage and usage of minutes and hours. Put a good, big, easily visible, "nagging" clock in every work area. If you spend a lot of time on the phone, have and use a timer.

Beyond simple awareness, there are practical strategies, methods, procedures, and tools that the busiest, most pressured person can use to crowbar some breathing room into his schedule, to force others to cooperate with his exceptional needs, to squeeze just a bit more out of each day. In this book, I give you mine. You will undoubtedly be interested in some, uninterested in others, maybe even repulsed by a few. That's OK. Although it's generally a bad idea to hire an advice-giver and then choose only the advice you like, in this case, it IS a cafeteria, and you can pick and choose and still get value.

Now it is time to get to work.

—Dan S. Kennedy

• • • • •

Note: The original, first edition of this book was written and published in 1996. Yes, way back then! During that elapsed time of some 17 years, 148,920 hours, 8,935,200 minutes, a lot has changed for me. I've ceased traveling like a maniac, dropping from an average 20 road-warrior days a month to four or five in some months, zero in most. To do this, I totally re-engineered my business. Also since the publication of the first edition of this book, I have been diagnosed with diabetes. I lost 45 pounds and have kept if off. To date, I have held the diabetes in check with nutrition, diet, exercise, and no prescription drugs. I've dramatically increased the time and energy given to another endeavor of mine—harness racing. I own, at any given time, parts or all of 16 to 30 racehorses, and I drive in races most weeks. I am also, of course, years closer to the 19th hole. To paraphrase Yogi, it's getting later earlier.

How has all this changed the attitudes and beliefs I express about time in this book? Not much at all. If anything, the passing of time has stiffened my resolve about safeguarding it, wisely investing it, enjoying it, and bringing wrath upon any who would steal it, waste it, or abuse it.

How has the passing of time changed my personal practices with regard to time? Only made them even more stringent, me more militant. I think I may have mellowed, gotten softer in other ways, but not when it comes to time. So this book accurately reflects my thoughts, my modus operandi today. It is absolutely applicable today, and, I think, more critically important than when first conceived.

An Invitation

Throughout this book, you will catch references to GKIC Insider's Circle and to the Members of this organization. If you are not familiar with this global association of entrepreneurs and the opportunities for business and personal growth it offers, please accept the invitation on page 187 of this book. There's no reason not to do it immediately. You need not complete this book first.

The big thing that has changed since this book's first publication is the large and growing number of my own clients, GKIC Insider's Circle Members, and readers of prior editions who've adopted—many, timidly, even fearfully, and skeptically at first—the advice in this book and lived to be grateful for doing so. When I first wrote the book, I was more of a lone wolf, but today thousands have adopted these methods and reported life-altering results.

I will welcome YOUR comments. You can fax me at 602-269-3113. No, you can't call me. Nor do I accept email. You'll read why in this book.

For Those Unfamiliar with Dan Kennedy, a Brief Description of His Motivations for Militant Safeguarding and Control of His Time, and a Few of His Most Interesting Procedures

For more than 25 years, Dan Kennedy traveled extensively, often exceeding 120 to 130 travel days a year, presenting as many as 70 speaking engagements and seminars annually. In addition, he consulted with numerous clients, ran as many as four businesses simultaneously, and employed as many as 42 people and as few as one. He also wrote and had published at least one new book a year, wrote and saw published more than 100 other books, audio programs, and home study courses; wrote and published two monthly newsletters the entire time; got involved in horse racing; and still took quite a few vacations every year.

Presently, he maintains a slightly saner schedule, notably with substantially reduced travel. Still, he has a stable of private clients, directs coaching/peer advisory groups, and he spends one day every month tele-coaching the same clients and groups. He writes direct-response ads and direct-mail copy for more than 20 clients a year, and has clients come to him for more than 30 consulting days a year. He writes five monthly newsletters, writes at least one book a year, and drives in harness races two or more nights a week almost every week. And he takes vacations.

He has but one staffperson, in an office distant from his own home office. He takes no unscheduled incoming calls, does not own a cell phone, and stubbornly refuses to use email. He deals with the majority of his faxes and mail only once each week.

Entrepreneurs have traveled from England, Australia, New Zealand, Japan, Korea, Mexico, Argentina, Russia, Canada, and every nook and cranny of the United States and paid $2,000.00 to $5,000.00 each to attend his intensive, multiday seminars on entrepreneurial success in which the subject of time is always addressed. Kennedy is legendary within his Insider's Membership and clientele of thousands for his unusual modus operandi concerning time. In this book, you get an inside look at the key strategies employed and the thinking of one of the most dedicated time and productivity managers to walk the earth!

It is significant that Kennedy is no longer alone in utilizing these methods—in fact, he has inspired countless business owners and sales professionals to make radical changes in the way they control their time access and that of the people around them.

> "Nothing is worth more than this day."
>
> —GOETHE

CHAPTER 1

How to Turn Time
Into Money

Eliminate the time between the idea and the act, and
your dreams will become realities.
—Dr. Edward L. Kramer, Inventor of the
Self-Improvement System Known as "Synchromatics"

W hat is "entrepreneurship" if not the conversion of
your knowledge, talent, and guts—through investment
of your time—into money?

Starting with the very next chapter, we dive into very
specific how-to strategies, but first I think you'll find it useful
to understand how I arrived at my philosophy of valuing time
and how I value time. I'll be the first to tell you, you can't eat
philosophy, but you do need your own philosophy of time
valuing.

In time management books and in time management
seminars, authors and speakers love to show off charts and graphs
depicting the dollar value of each workday hour, depending on
your income or the income you want to achieve. Maybe you've

sat through one of these little graph-and-pointer sessions before. You know, Mr. Lecturer up there, laptop computer wired into the overhead projector, lights dimmed, even a laser beam pointer in hand so he can show off his beautiful five-color bar graph. If you use his numbers, for example, based on eight-hour workdays, presuming 220 workdays, earning $200,000.00 a year requires that each hour be worth $113.64.

Unfortunately, it's all a pile of seminar room B.S.

Here's why: It's all based on eight-hour workdays. Eight hours a day. But there's not a soul on the planet who gets in eight *productive* hours a day. Not even close. You see, the workday hour is one thing, *the productive hour*—or what I call the billable hour—is another. Elsewhere in this book, there's a definition of productivity you may want to use to determine which of your hours are productive.

Now, if you happen to be an attorney, none of this matters. It seems lawyers bill out hours whether productive or not. Here's a joke. A 35-year-old lawyer in perfect health suddenly drops dead. He gets to Saint Peter at The Gate and argues, "You guys screwed up. You pulled me up here early." Saint Peter checks his clipboard and says, "No, sir. Judging by your total billable hours, you're 113 years old and we're late." *Lawyers*.

But the rest of us can only collect on genuinely productive hours.

Can One "Number" Change Your Life?

Let's go back to the math game and assume that $200,000.00 is your base earnings target. (We'll talk more about what that term means later.) How many of your hours will be productive, directly generating revenue? How many will be otherwise consumed: commuting, filling out government paperwork, dealing with vendors, emptying the trash cans (I hope not), whatever? Let's say it is one-third productive, two-thirds other. That's pretty generous. One study of Fortune 500 CEOs revealed they averaged 28 productive minutes a day. The business legend Lee Iacocca, who made the Mustang happen at Ford and who rescued Chrysler from the brink of bankruptcy in the 1980s with minivans and cup holders and bold warranties, personally told me he figured top CEOs might squeeze in 45 productive minutes per day—the rest of the day fighting off time-wasting B.S. like a frantic fellow futilely waving his arms at a swarm of angry bees on attack. It must be even worse today, given the explosion of time-intruding technology. But let's generously make 33% of your time productive. With that, only one of three hours counts as "billable." So you've got to multiply the $113.64 times three, $340.92. This becomes your governing number for $200,000.00 a year. For $600,000.00, three times that: $1,022.76.

When I wrote the first edition of this book in 1996, I was charging about $3,500.00 to write an advertising campaign for a client. By the time I updated this book in 2004, that fee had multiplied five times. Today, a full campaign bills at $75,000.00 to $150,000.00 plus royalties. Since the time required is about the same, if not less, as my memory bank of material and proficiency have grown, this puts more and more weight on any time wasted. So the ideas and methods I describe in this book are a lot more important to me today than they were in 1996 or in 2004. Of course, it's arguably true that I can more easily afford to repel some clients and annoy some people with these methods now than then, but I contend I got here, in part, by thinking about time in this fashion and doing these things long before I could ostensibly afford them.

Anyway, let's roll back the calendar and assume I currently charge a client $3,500.00, and that my base earnings target number requires an hourly average of $340.92. If you travel in business, you have to think about this a lot. I once lived in Arizona, and often traveled for business. I currently have homes in Ohio and in Virginia, grew to loathe travel, and now do it as little as possible. I insist the clients, coaching groups, even events I speak at occur in my home cities. But when I was traveling, if there were two days of travel bracketing a day of work, that put three days' cost to that work. Using the $340.92 hourly number, that's $8,182.08 of cost.

Few people ever factor cost of their time (or their staff's time) into product, service, deliverable cost, or the maintenance of each client of variable value, or much of anything else. But you should. At just $340.92 an hour, a client who comes to you costs only for the hours he is there. A client you must drive an hour to visit and hour to return from costs $683.84 more. If that's four times a year, one costs $2,735.36 more than the other. Consider two customers, each worth $3,000.00 a year, but one is needier and more demanding than the other. One consumes eight hours, the other three. The first may not even be worth having, particularly if there are enough of the second to be had. This, by the way, is why I book 20-minute, not 30-minute, calls with my coaching clients. I can do three per hour at 20 minutes each but only three per 1½ hours at 30 minutes each. In a year, 10 minutes saved per month per client = two hours! Times 20 clients, a full week!

So, again, let's say my number is $340.92, calendar rolled back. Here's how I have to use it.

First, it has to be on my mind constantly. Is what I'm doing worth $340.92 an hour to do it?

Second, it puts a meter on others' consumption of my time—that unnecessary 12-minute phone conversation just cost $68.18. Same with 12 minutes at Facebook or Twitter. This exercise forces you to think of time and activity in terms of investment and expense. It enables you to quantify what is going on in your life.

Third, for me it sets the base cost for hours given to a speaking engagement, consulting assignment, copywriting assignment, and other things I do that are directly billable. And if you do anything but earn a fixed salary, you have to weigh this base cost against every activity, to set your fee or to decide whether or not to bother.

I've learned to think about time cost and time cost of travel a lot. When I first started shifting from going to clients to getting clients to travel to me, I used differential pricing. At that time, a consulting day billed at $8,300.00 if I came to you but only $7,800.00 if you came to me. Why? Because it's worth money to me to stay home, be able to write for an hour in the morning before the consulting day, finish and be at home at 4:30, be able to drive in harness races and not miss any, sleep in my own bed, and be at work in my home office promptly at 7:00 A.M. the next morning vs. losing that hour the day of and losing a half day or so to travel on either side. Gradually I eliminated the differential pricing and simply mandated that clients travel to me. I finally converted to flying only by private jet, and that exorbitant expense to be absorbed by a client has pretty much ended any discussion of me coming to them. In a way, that expense added to fees has re-created differential pricing; even the cost of the client plus a couple staff people traveling commercial to me is a lot lower than my fee plus my private jet bill. Looked at side by side on a sheet of paper, it's dramatic—if the client fails to factor in the dollar value of his and his staff's travel time. Which most clients do not. Differential pricing is useful for a variety of purposes. Within GKIC, there are lawyers, accountants, dentists, and others who charge a higher fee if they do a client's work than they do if they only supervise the work done by subordinates.

You don't have to be flying the unfriendly skies to do travel time cost math. Many years ago, when I was in the field selling, I quickly figured out that you could fit in two, three, four, or five appointments per day, depending on how you routed yourself. A salesman half as good at selling as a competitor but twice as good at efficiently routing himself and clustering prospects makes the same amount of money. With this in mind, I've long "clustered" as much productive activity as possible if traveling or even when leaving the house. We'll talk more about that in Chapter 6. By not "clustering," most people allow a great deal of inefficiency to sneak into their lives.

By working at home, as a writer, consultant, and tele-coach, as opposed to going to an office, I make a lot of money each day just by not commuting. I have conditioned myself to go directly from bed to shower to work in 15 minutes. If I were leaving the house to go to an office, I'd have those 15 minutes plus another half hour, maybe an hour, commute, then another 15 minutes getting settled in at the office. Not to mention the commute at end of day.

Seek LEVERAGE

In whatever ways you can in your business, you need to seek leverage. In terms of work productivity, leverage is, in essence, the difference between the base cost for your hour and the amount of money you get for it or from it. One good way to evaluate your personal effectiveness is measuring and monitoring this differential, hour by hour, for a week.

Now, let's go back to the term *base earning target*. Since you are your own boss, you write your own paycheck, and you decide how much that paycheck is going to be. For most entrepreneurs, that number is—whatever's left! This is a huge mistake, for two reasons: It indicates zero planning, and it means you pay yourself last, the number-one reason entrepreneurs wind up broke. So, let's reverse all that, and start with the planning. You've got to decide how much money you're going to take out of your business or businesses this year in salary, perks, contributions to retirement plans, and so on. What is that number?

I'll tell you this: eight out of ten entrepreneurs I ask
cannot come up with this number.

Anyway, if you do not have a base income target, then you cannot calculate what your time must be worth, which means you cannot make good decisions about the investment of your time, which means you are not exercising any real control over your business or life at all. You are a wandering generality. Is that what you want to do—*just wander around and settle for whatever you get?*

Now, you may not have a situation that lends itself to clear-cut billable hours as I do, so how can this strategy work for you? *It has to.* It's even more important to you than to me. Let's say you own six stores. Each store has a manager. Hey, this is complicated. Well, you'll have to decide how much of the business's bottom-line profit goal will be provided by the managers whether you sleep or work and how much is still inextricably linked to you. If you want $500,000.00 at the bottom line and you figure half is dependent on you, you've got a $250,000.00 target.

> *E*ntrepreneurs should think about the purpose of business. A lot of business owners lose sight of that altogether. The purpose of a business is to make its owner rich. The first responsibility of the owner is to extract money from the business, not leave it locked up in it or, worse, put money into it.

For me, it's reasonably precise. For you, it may not be such an exact science. But that's OK. I promise you that coming up with a number, even if it is arrived at through some pretty questionable calculations, is still a whole lot better than not having a number at all. Having a number is going to make such a dramatic change in so many of the decisions you make, habits you cultivate, and people you associate with that the benefits will be so extraordinary it won't matter if the original method of getting to a number had a technical flaw or two buried in it. At least for the sake of our conversation in this book, get a number. YOUR base earnings target for the next full calendar year (see Figure 1.1). Divide it by the number of workday hours. Multiply it to allow for unproductive vs. productive hours. If you haven't a better estimate of that, use the three-time multiple I've used here. Now you have what your time is supposed to be worth per hour. Divided by 60, per minute.

That little number may just change your life.

It's sort of like a heart attack—or, in my own case, a diabetes diagnosis—being required to really get somebody to change their eating and exercise habits.

FIGURE 1.1: Calculating Your Base Earnings Target

Base earnings target: $_____

Divided by (220 days x 8 = 1,760)
work hours in a year   ÷_____

= base hourly number $_____

Times productivity vs. nonproductivity
multiple   X_____

_____

= What your time must be worth per hour: $_____

A lot of your decision-making gets easy with this number staring you in the face. It's hard to con yourself with this number staring you in the face. In fact, I suggest having it stare you in the face a lot until you internalize it. Write your number, "$____ Per Hour," on a bunch of colorful 4 x 6-inch cards in bold black letters, and stick these cards up in places where you work and will see them often.

Generally speaking, two business life changes probably come to mind immediately, with this number staring you in the face:

First, you realize that you've got to surround yourself with people who understand and respect the value of your time and behave accordingly. This is not easy. And they will forget, over time. Familiarity breeds contempt. Periodically, you will have to re-orient them. You also must get people who do not respect the value of your time out of your business life. If you let people who do not understand and respect the value of your time hang around, you won't have a fighting chance.

Dan Kennedy's #1 No B.S. Time Truth

If you don't know what your time is worth, you can't expect the world to know it either.

Second, you have to eliminate the need for doing tasks and activities that just cannot and do not match up with the mandated value of your time or delegate them.

How Low Can You Go in Valuing Time?

I grew up in Ohio, where people spend their weekends shoveling snow in the winter, cutting grass in the spring and summer, and raking leaves in the fall. It used to make me crazy to drive around and see somebody in my sales organization out shoveling, mowing, or raking. I'd say if your time isn't worth more than the $5 an hour you could give some neighborhood kid to do this, you should be shot. Plus, you're robbing some kid out of the money. When I moved to Arizona, I envisioned sand, rocks, and cactus—nothing to shovel or mow. Guess what? A bunch of folks bring grass with 'em and stick it everywhere, then alternate between watering it and mowing it. Others, with "desert landscaping," can be found out there raking their gravel—like cats in litter boxes! What conclusion did I draw from all that? Most people will find ways to avoid confronting productivity and will waste their time, even if they have to work at it!

Well, my "philosophy of time valuing" can be boiled down to this: Every one of my working hours has to be worth a certain amount of money. I do everything I can to create and protect that value; and anybody screwing that up had better watch out.

Another, related issue is "project valuing" or "opportunity valuing" or "account valuing" for salespeople. In short, a "thing" has to be worth X dollars, whatever you decide X must be, for you to even touch it, think about it, or be involved with it. Many of my best clients have adopted this idea and now have their own litmus test, helpful in quickly and decisively saying yea or nay to whatever comes along.

Most sales professionals hang onto clients and accounts that consume far, far more time than they can ever be worth. Better to send them to a competitor. Most entrepreneurs perpetuate projects that consume far, far more time—theirs or employees'—than they're worth. I've done it more times than I care to confess. But I'm getting much better at NOT doing it with each passing year. As a good reminder, my friend Lee Milteer, a top business performance coach and the host interviewer on my Renegade Millionaire System audio program, gave me a wall plaque as my 49th birthday gift that reads:

Dan's Other Business

It Seemed Like a Good Idea
At the Time, Inc.

Temptations

Success and productivity are not the same things, nor does maximum productivity necessarily translate to success. You might, for example, achieve a very high level of productivity at cold-call prospecting and pushing through CEOs' doors in order to sell your services, but come to understand that you do not feel at all successful as a result. Instead, perpetually stressed and anxious, demeaned by the "numbers game" and the rejection, burnt-out, and you come to realize you would have been better served devoting productive energy to building a marketing system that brought interested prospects to you.

As you set out to get a far stronger grip on your time, to enhance your performance, it's important to be constantly assessing your reasons for doing so and the validity of the objectives you are pursuing and achieving.

Temptations, continued

Entrepreneurs tend to be under more constant assault than executives or others, so it is easier to lose grip on the thread that leads through the muddle to the prize. Prizes you don't really want get set up in front of you by others, and you race to get to them while losing the critical thinking that questions the appropriateness of the prize. This takes your time and invests it where it can't get a desirable return. Entrepreneurs are, by conditioned habit, often by ingrained compulsion, perhaps even by nature, Problem Solvers and Mountain Climbers. It's what we do. But not every problem is one you need to solve or should care about solving. Not every mountain you are led to needs to be conquered by you.

My racehorses are incapable of critical thinking. They are bred and trained and conditioned nearly from birth to race. They are noble and fierce and *automatic* competitors. When I climb into the sulky and drive the horse to the track, get him moving behind the starting gate amongst the other horses, never, never, never does he stop and think—*gee, maybe this is a race I don't need to run.* But you and I are capable of such critical thinking. We can rein ourselves in. As entrepreneurs, we are automatic competitors, automatic problem solvers, automatic mountain climbers—but we are capable of overriding our automatic inclinations.

If you put a business problem or opportunity in front of a true entrepreneur, he automatically leaps upon it and begins solving it or capitalizing on it. He reacts as if a lion thrown a hunk of raw, red meat. The lion will respond even if he has just had a big meal and is not hungry. The entrepreneur will respond even if he has more on his plate than he can handle, no need to respond,

Temptations, continued

no time to respond. In this way, entrepreneurs are dangerous to themselves.

You can reduce that danger with more disciplined time management. With entire weeks scheduled and scripted in advance, the new and unexpected must take a place in line, patiently wait, and instead of reacting impulsively, you can attend to it more calmly and thoughtfully. One of my principles is that nothing is ever as bad or as good as it initially appears. Before acting hastily based on first impressions, each new thing—problem or opportunity— must be carefully inspected.

CHAPTER 2

How to Drive a Stake Through
the Hearts of the Time Vampires
Out to Suck You Dry

And even as they looked the thing tore the throat out of Hugo Baskerville, on
which, as it turned its blazing eyes and ripping jaws upon them,
the three shrieked with fear and rode for dear life, still
screaming, across the moor.

—FROM *THE HOUND OF THE BASKERVILLES* BY SIR ARTHUR CONAN DOYLE

I n recent years, vampires have enjoyed a resurgence
of popularity in America. They're right up there with the
Kardashians. Teenage girls—and some adult women—are
swooning over them at the movies, on TV, and in books. But
there is nothing romantic about TIME Vampires.

Time vampires are needy, thirsty, selfish, vicious creatures
who, given an opportunity, will suck up all of your time and
energy, leaving you white, weak, and debilitated. Once they
have found a good meal, they start coming back every day. Even
though you regenerate yourself with a meal, a night's sleep, and
a vial of vitamins, it's to no avail. They will be waiting for you
tomorrow just where they left you yesterday, eager to once again
suck every ounce of life from your veins. Being able to recognize

these vampires on sight is the first step in protecting yourself from them. Being willing to deal with them as you would a vile, evil, blood-sucking creature of the dark is the first step in freeing yourself from them.

Got a Minute?

Maybe the most insidious of all the Time Vampires is *Mr. Have-You-Got-a-Minute*? He lurks in the shadows in the hall outside your office, near the elevator, near the cafeteria, in the bushes next to the parking lot, wherever it is possible to catch you off guard. If you give in to him a few times, he becomes emboldened and starts "dropping in" to your office or home. He disarms you with "Have you got a minute?" or "I just need a couple minutes of your time" or "I just have one quick question." He has a unique knack of pulling this stunt right when you are in the middle of doing something incredibly important—getting mentally prepared for a most important phone call or at some similar moment. If you are in his vicinity all day, he'll also "drop by" a dozen times a day—each time needing "just a minute."

This Time Vampire can also drain your blood at a distance. The equivalent of loitering in your office doorway with "just a quick question" is the random email or text message. I say random because it is. Any time, every time this vampire has a thought, he sends an email. Any time, every time he has a question—why go look something up or figure it out?—he texts you. Unpunished, he'll drop by this way 3 times, 6 times, 20 times a day.

Each time he drops by, picture him sinking his teeth into your neck and sucking out a pint or two. That IS the effect he has.

The temptation to give in to this particular vampire is almost irresistible. First of all, it just seems easier to deal with his "one quick question" immediately than to put him off and have it hanging over you for later. Second, it *feels* rude and unreasonable to refuse him. But the truth is, he deserves no courtesy whatsoever. He is telling you that your time is less valuable than his, that whatever you are doing is unimportant and easily interrupted. He is, in street jargon, dissing you to the max. So, go ahead and stick a stake through his heart without a moment's remorse.

Here's the stake.

I'm busy right now.
Let's meet at 4:00 P.M. for 15 minutes,
and tackle everything on your list at one time.

This stops this bloodthirsty vampire in his tracks. Freezes him, like a deer in headlights. Next, it "teaches" this vampire a new discipline. Of course, he won't get it the first time. Or the second. He'll keep trying for a while. But if you whip out this same stake every time, over and over again, and jam it firmly through his chest, eventually he *will* get the message. Someday, he'll call you and say something like: "I have five things I need to go over with you. When can we get together?" After you pick yourself up off the floor, you can congratulate yourself on having defanged and housebroken a vampire.

As to the many missives from a distance blood-sucker, I largely prevent this bad behavior by refusing to be personally connected to the internet, use email, own a cell phone, or text at all. My time fortress is free of these holes in its wall. But when somebody tries it with the only communication methods I allow—faxes and phone calls to my assistant—I stick a stake in them damn fast. I teach clients, associates, vendors, and others 1) to organize their thoughts and questions and communicate sparingly, about everything at once—not incessantly, about one thing at a time, and 2) to expect delayed response.

"They're In a Meeting"

The next most dangerous Time Vampire is *Mr. Meeting.* Some people seem to do nothing but attend meetings. Just as I was finishing this book, a client of mine dragged me into a 20-minute, four-person conference call to discuss when we could have the next, longer conference call to plan a meeting. Geez.

Being in meetings is *seductive.* It is a way to feel important. It's also a great way to hide from making and taking responsibility for decisions. *Meetingitis* is a disease that turns businesses into unproductive, indecisive, slow-moving coffee klatches. (The two toughest CEOs I know hold only "stand-up meetings." No chairs.)

It is my observation that this situation has only worsened year after year. Even though we've all been offered, and most have accepted, a whole new arsenal of gadgets and technologies that are supposed to make communication more efficient, everybody I try to connect with is *in a meeting.*

The other day, I called a company, pressed for some information, and got this from the frazzled receptionist: "Everybody's in meetings. I don't know anything. Please call back some other time when there might be somebody who knows something available."

You need to stop and ask yourself do I really need to be in—or hold—this meeting? Is there a more time-efficient way to handle this? A conference call? A memo circulated to each person? Heck, a posting on a bulletin board. Or an internet site. An email. Hey, anything BUT another meeting.

If you are going to hold a meeting, there are several stakes you can use to stop the vampires from making it an endless "blood klatch." (Time Vampires love meetings because a bunch of blood-rich victims gather in one place at one time. It's like a buffet.)

1. Set the meeting for immediately before lunch or at the end of the day, so the vampires are eager to get it done and over with, turn into bats, and fly out of there.
2. Don't serve refreshments.
3. Circulate a written agenda in advance.
4. Have and communicate a clear, achievable objective for the meeting.

This refreshment thing's a big tip, by the way. My friend Dave Petito, a great TV infomercial producer, and I both used to get paid to attend meetings for the same company. These took place at the firm's palatial Beverly Hills office or sometimes its CEO's home. Either place, the table was laden end to end with a fabulous array of food: bagels, five flavors of cream cheese, salmon, imported cheeses, sandwich meats, croissants, muffins, cookies. Really good grub. Added at least an hour or more to every meeting. After all, you can't advise with your mouth full. This company has long since gone out of business. I wonder why.

If you must attend a meeting, you also have some stakes available so you can slay Mr. Meeting.

1. Determine in advance what information you are to contribute, then do it with a prepared, minimum-time, maximum-impact presentation.
2. Have an exit strategy: someone coming in to get you at a certain time, a pre-arranged call on your cell phone, whatever. You can then excuse yourself only long enough to make a call and return if you need to—but you probably won't.

Playing Trivial Pursuit

Another Time Vampire to watch out for is *Mr. Trivia*. He either can't or doesn't want to differentiate between the important and unimportant, minor and major.

This vampire's talent is getting others off track, getting you to set aside your carefully organized list of priorities in favor of his, and more often than not, his agenda will be of minimal importance. Mr. Trivia will interrupt to tell you just about anything, ranging from the building being on fire to the office supply store having delivered blue pens instead of black pens. Usually it'll be the latter.

The best way to deal with this one is to drop a big silver cross around his neck and kick him off the parapet of your castle. But failing the opportunity of doing that, you need another stake. This one is to interrupt the interrupter:

I have an exceptionally busy day, so I am only dealing with
9s and 10s on a 1–10 scale. Everything else
MUST wait until tomorrow.
Are you convinced that what you want to talk
to me about is a 9 or 10?

He will say, "No, but—" and then you must again rudely interrupt him: "No buts. Thanks. We'll get to it tomorrow." Then physically get away. (If he's in YOUR office, you leave.)

He will be offended. Good. The odds of him holding the trivial matter over until tomorrow and bringing it back to you are less than 50-50. He'll go sink his teeth into somebody else's throat. Or maybe even resolve it on his own. But he *won't* patiently wait until tomorrow.

Oh Boy, It's Soap Opera Time

Have you ever watched soap opera diva Susan Lucci overact? I believe the show *All My Children* finally ended its 40 years on air a couple years ago, also ending Susan's histrionics. Such drama queen overreaction is the hallmark of all great soap opera stars. Someone can walk into a room and say, "Ronald has just been murdered and is lying outside on the lawn with a giant metal pink flamingo stuck through his chest," or walk in and say, "It's raining outside," and get the same massive reaction: crying, sobbing, pulling hair, chest heaving, body twisting, overacting.

Well, some people are just like soap opera stars in real life. They turn everything into an emotional crisis. They react to everything emotionally. They magnify everything's importance. And if you're not careful, they'll pull you right into the drama. When they do, visualize them sticking in the IV and taking out a quart.

The other problem with these particular vampires is that, at the very least, they make you give up your time to attempt to put them back together emotionally. They guilt you into giving them your shoulder to cry on. And while they're resting their head on your shoulder, they're sinking their teeth into your neck.

Some people have the amazing ability to turn every molehill into a mountain. If you happen to have some of these overactive, emotionally wrought weepers in your organization, get rid of them if you can. If you can't do that, then personally stay away from them. There are two ways to drive them away.

1. Cut to the core of their problem (which is usually glaringly obvious) and tell them what to do. This is not what they want. They don't want solutions; they want soap opera. Spoil their fun and they'll go looking for blood elsewhere.
2. Take over the conversation by launching into a long, boring, pointless story; say: "That reminds me of a time when my Uncle Harold was in the Dust Bowl during the Great Depression. This story will help you. Here goes!" In other words, turn into a vampire yourself and start sucking.

Are There Other Time Vampires?

There are almost as many different varieties of Time Vampires as there are birds or butterflies. Your productivity multiplies as you get better and better skilled at spotting them and driving stakes through their hearts.

Ask yourself if you're doing something now to invite the time vampires in for a feast. If so, stop doing it.

How I Stupidly Put Out the Welcome Mat for the Time Vampires and Let Them Suck Me Dry

In an article I read in some business magazine, a story was told of how a brave CEO, in one of his first acts as president of a medical center, yanked his office door from its hinges and suspended it from the lobby ceiling to demonstrate his commitment to an open-door policy. This was applauded by the magazine as some giant act of courage and creativity. I chuckled when I read this. This guy has my sympathy. To the management theorists who get all wet and excited when they hear this sort of thing, I say, "C'mon out into the real world, where they eat their young every day, and try this yourself. You won't last a week."

This tactic is nothing new or revolutionary or innovative. Heck, I made that same mistake about 30 years ago.

Right after I took the helm of a barely afloat manufacturing company, I pried the office door off the hinges, nailed it to

Dan Kennedy's #2 No B.S. Time Truth

Time Vampires will suck as much blood out of you as you permit. If you're drained dry at day's end, it's your fault.

the wall sideways, and proclaimed that, from now on, the president's office had a true "open-door policy." High drama. Incredible stupidity.

All day long, an endless parade of Time Vampires. Suck, suck, suck. By the end of the day, my neck looked like a pincushion. I was whiter than typing paper. Almost transparent. Slumped over my desk, not even enough energy left to sit upright. Eyes glazed over. Breathing shallow. I'm telling you, they just lined up, marched in, and happily took turns siphoning me dry. The only thing that stopped them from slicing me up like London Broil and consuming me completely was the clock reaching 5:00 P.M. I put out the vampire welcome mat, and they took me up on the invitation. My fault, of course.

This sort of thing looks just great on paper. Unfortunately, a lot of ideas—like this one—is put on paper by goofball authors (!) who haven't a lick of real-world experience, have their butts safely parked on a bucolic college campus somewhere, and have a ball dreaming up clever-sounding psychobabble buzzwords and hot, new management theories to baffle and bedazzle us with. Well, don't believe everything you read.

Before You Can Win, You Have to Hate to Lose

The great, then pretty much crazed Oakland Raider Howie Long, now a Fox Sports commentator, said that before a team can consistently win, its players must truly, deeply, viscerally, violently hate losing. Howie reportedly yanked a locker door off its hinges and stood there chewing its metal after a losing game. More than once.

Letting Time Vampires steal even a spoonful of your blood has to be looked at as *losing,* and you have to truly hate it before you can win at safeguarding and maximizing the gains and benefits from your time.

I have not mellowed at this. In fact, the older I get, and the less time I know I have before The End, the more I hate, and I mean *hate,* having my time wasted. Referring back to the calculations of Chapter 1 can assist you with building up a resentment for Time Vampires' blood-sucking, but I urge going beyond that, being more emotional and enraged about it. These Time Vampires are evil. Often they know full well what they are doing, and that fact says they have disdain and disrespect for you. They are declared enemies. Thieves. If their bad behavior is thoughtless, the damage is the same, and their thoughtlessness is the evil.

I've yet to meet a successful entrepreneur or sales professional who wasn't competitive, but the great ones are fiercely competitive. They hate losing. In business, and in anything, however losing is defined, this is how you must view your war with Time Vampires. Either they win and you lose or you win and they lose. It is a competition, a test of wills.

CHAPTER 3

Stopping "Productivus Interruptus" Once and For All

Mail, faxes, email, texts, tweets, calls and more,
and a parade of people at the door
at all hours, uncontrolled, in they pour
Your intentions, your agenda in tatters on the floor
In your pantry, but a meager store.

I nterruptions destroy many office- or desk-bound individuals' productivity.

Put a stop to interruptions, multiply your productivity. It is that simple.

After reading a study claiming that the average business owner is interrupted once every eight minutes, I had three of my clients who spend all day on their business premises put a watch on it for a day. One reported a better average: once per ten. The other two, six, and the third hollered, "Hey, I need a stopwatch."

When I used to go to my offices in a place where I was under the same roof with my staff, I found that to be about par—*if I let it happen*. And, as a big thumb rule, the more employees or associates you've got, the more you get interrupted. Some years back, I suddenly wound up with a staff of 42 people thrust upon me. For a while I was interrupted every eight *seconds*, not every eight minutes. It was embarrassing to ultimately realize that this was all my fault. I permitted, even invited the interruptions. And I learned to stop them.

There are many reasons for these interruptions, and almost none of them have to do with necessity! If you're going to achieve peak personal productivity in such an environment, here are the five self-defense, time-defense tactics you'll have to use:

1. Get lost.
2. Don't answer the phone.
3. Get a grip on email, texts, and faxes.
4. Set the timer on the bomb.
5. Be busy and be obvious about it.

Get Lost

Your first tactic—simple inaccessibility. When I was in the office, I got asked lots of questions that I knew the people figured out for themselves when I wasn't there, so my being there, and being accessible, actually diminished *their* productivity as well as mine. The answer is not to be there at all. Some entrepreneurs think they have to set a leadership example by being the first person there, to turn on the lights, and the last person to leave, to turn off the lights. I made this mistake, and it IS a huge mistake. Leadership is *not* about outworking everybody.

I learned by traveling that my people functioned just as well or better with me as an absentee leader as they did with me onsite. When I was on the road and inaccessible, they handled 80% of everything on their own, most of it satisfactorily, some with excellence, and a little bit unsatisfactorily but almost always repairable. And they asked me about the other 20% quickly and efficiently, in brief phone conversations or via a fax waiting for me at my hotel. Since that worked okay when it had to, there's no reason it couldn't work all the time. So I stopped going in to the office—period. I had a fax at home and at the office, so when I was in town, I stayed at home and worked there largely uninterrupted. When necessary, I faxed or phoned in and they phoned or faxed me.

Today, I live and work at my Ohio home more than anywhere else. I have only one staff person, and she is in the office—in Phoenix. About as far from underfoot as can be. Almost without exception, we talk by phone once a day, usually for less than 20 minutes. I get truly urgent faxes once a day; and once a week I get a nicely organized box of other faxes, mail, and a list of questions. She is far better organized in dealing with me than she'd be were I there or more accessible. I am far better organized in dealing with her. I'm certain it equates to at least two hours of productivity saved per day for both of us, and in my world, that's a whole pile of money. A lot more than the weekly FedEx bill.

I have used this method for ten years, and it has served me well. I have seen no reason to expand the range of ways people can gain access to me—and plenty of reasons not to.

People often complain to me about being so overwhelmed with in-bound and accumulated email they face it with dread. Sometimes they just desperately delete everything, thus missing out on communication or information of significance to them. They complain about the frequent interruptions by email and text, and the pressure of others' expectations of instant response. In truth, they are enabling terrorism. I explain that I am never victimized by any of this—and they shake their heads in wonderment. At a recent seminar where each person was given the opportunity of asking just one burning question that puzzled them most about me, an owner of several businesses asked,

"How can you possibly do all that you do without email?" I answered that I was able to do all that I do precisely because I refuse to participate in email.

I know you will consider all this radical and out of step, and have 20 quick reasons why you could never restrict access so severely. Truth be told, the biggest problem you would have would be purely emotional: not being able to handle the ribbing and criticism. Dozens and dozens of my clients have mimicked my practices, and been shocked by how much more productive they've become. These include people in diverse businesses and sales careers, with small and large staffs, running businesses from $1 million to $30 million in size. The owner of one of these good-sized companies has gone from five days a week at the office to zero, instead working at his lakeside home or beachfront condo, in near isolation, and conducting business with staff and clients by preset phone meeting appointments, clumped into one day a week. He's been getting so much more accomplished this way that he's cut his hours devoted to that business by one-third, doubled his income, and greatly improved his health to boot, with newfound time for exercise.

I have a friend, a CEO of a $4 or $5 million-a-year business, who can't work at home; he has six kids, two dogs, one spouse.

Dan Kennedy's #3 No B.S. Time Truth

If they can't find you,
they can't interrupt you.

So he has a small $200-a-month office in town, about halfway between his home and his manufacturing facility. It has no phone and no fax. And he spends most of his time there.

Another business owner I know has been weaning his staff from him and weaning himself from being in his office every minute, poking his nose in everything, second-guessing everybody. To his shock and surprise, things have been going well. A few people in his organization have risen to the occasion. A few have proven unable to adjust and been fired. Overall, sales and profits are up. He is finding time to invent and work on "special projects" he's been thinking about for years. And for the first time ever, he's taking an entire month of vacation, at a rented beach cottage, several states away from his business. For the first time in 30 years, he's really becoming a business owner instead of being owned by a business.

If you *are* going to be in your office with the rest of your staff, then, contrary to my dumb open door management experiment, it is very important that you have a CLOSED DOOR POLICY. You need some times when everybody knows—because of the closed door, red light, stuffed purple dragon in the hallway, whatever—that you are 100% uninterruptible. And if you want to sit in there and take a nap, you go right ahead. It's none of their damned business.

Don't Answer the Phone

Next, you've got to get control over the telephone. The smartphone is supposed to be liberating. For most people, it is a leash. Its constant presence has made people's addiction to and desperation about instantly responding to the bell (or ring tone) worse than ever. By any and every phone, fools are intimidated and ruled, interrupted and distracted and derailed, bedeviled and stressed.

I think the phone is Peak Productivity Enemy Number One, and your people will be in cahoots with it until you break them of the habit. People somehow get conditioned that they must respond to the phone when it rings, and believe you should too. At home, on their own time, people will run dripping from the bathtub, jump up from the dinner table, even "coitus interruptus" to answer the phone. It's incredible how cowed by Mr. Bell's invention most people are. Ring. Run. Respond. *Nuts.*

So, first, let me offer a bit of philosophy: You have absolutely no legal, moral, or other responsibility to answer the phone or take a call unless you want to. At home, I routinely take the phone off the hook to take a shower, eat a meal, take a nap, watch a favorite TV program, or, well, for other things too. There's nothing—and I mean nothing—happening on earth that can't or won't wait an hour. Or two. You should also carry that attitude into your work. Different people need different levels of control over telephone interruptions, but I do not believe anybody ought to be wide open to inbound calls. This is like walking around with a "Kick Me" sign tacked to your back. If you take inbound calls as they come, you are constantly stopping work on a task of known priority in favor of something or someone of unknown priority. You are turning control of your day over to the unknown. And at the end of most days, you'll be worn out, but you won't have gotten to do most of the things you wanted to do.

Personally, I have very rarely encountered an inbound call damaged by a day's delay in response. Most of my inbound calls are fielded by voice mail, then my assistant, and almost never randomly or spontaneously returned by me. I haven't played phone tag in years. If the matter requires conversation with me, a phone appointment is set, for a specific number of minutes, with an end time, often with a delay of at least days to weeks before it occurs. Guess what? Occasionally, somebody's aggravated—which is their problem, not mine—but I have yet to notice this approach costing me any money. Not a nickel. In fact, ironically, in my business (and in many), being somewhat difficult to get to actually helps rather than hinders securing new clients and having those clients appreciate and respect your time and assistance. Rightly or wrongly, most folks don't put a lot of value on getting to the wise man at the bottom of the mountain. (I talk about this, in the context of "Takeaway Selling," in my book *No B.S. Sales Success in the New Economy.*)

The Take-with-You Phone

Now, the cell phone—an evil invention if there ever was one. People really feel compelled to answer these things 24/7. It is the ultimate interruption welcome mat, and it has amazing, mysterious powers over its owner.

As comedian Dennis Miller says, I don't want to get off on a rant here, but . . . increasingly, I am noticing men standing at urinals in public restrooms taking care of business while talking on the phone simultaneously. Look, if you can't even pee in peace, you are not Mr. Super-Important. You are Mr. Super-Stupid.

Personally, I refuse to own or use one at all. I had one for two weeks once. Wound down the car window one day and threw it as far as I could. Never been tempted again.

If you insist on carrying one of these miserable things, have the good sense to turn it off. A lot. Like to walk to lunch with coworkers or friends, eat, and actually digest what you eat. Or pee. Or, say, navigate your SUV down the side of a mountain, on an icy, curvy road. And have the common decency to turn it off and shut up when you are seated next to me in a theater, tight-quarters restaurant, or other public venue before I ram it down your throat.

This should be like smoking. It's at least as offensive. There should be a little glass room here and there, like smokers are stuck in at airports, where everybody who has to yap into their phone can go and be wedged in and annoy each other, leaving those of us with our lives under control and some sense of civility in peace. The pay phone in a booth was a wonderfully civilized thing. (I also favor a mandatory death penalty for texting while driving.)

In my seminars, by the way, we assess a $100.00 fine anytime a cell phone erupts. And confiscate the offending phone for the duration.

Often, the offenders have paid $2,000.00 to $5,000.00 to be in the room. Many are also very good clients. I don't care. I will

"It keeps me from looking at my phone every two seconds."

©2013 Walsh/The New Yorker Collection/www.cartoonbank.com

not tolerate it. I warn everybody, I put some big, beefy bruiser in charge of collecting, and I take the money. If you can't have your life sufficiently in order to pay uninterrupted attention and be courteous to others, I'd prefer you stay home and annoy someone else. I think restaurants and theaters ought to collect them when you come in and give them back when you leave, like civilized saloons did with gunslingers' weapons in the Old West.

And a word to business owners, salespeople, and my pathetically desperate and paranoid speaking colleagues who devoutly believe they must be instantly accessible at any and every moment to every client and prospective client to prevent that client from dialing the next number and doing business with whomever answers instantly. If you are that interchangeable, that mundane and ordinary a commodity, you've got big, big problems, far bigger than you can solve by answering your cell while you're on the can. Turn off the thing long enough to read my books *No B.S. Sales Success in The New Economy* and *No B.S. Guide to Trust-Based Marketing*. That's urgent.

I want to be emphatic on this point: If your clients, customers, or patients, and prospective clients, customers, or patients view you as one of and the same as many, so that if you aren't instantly accessible or responsive, whoever's next by alphabet or Google Local or whatever reference will do just as well, you have lost. You will suffer and die in the marketplace. Suffering such low status with clientele destroys your ability to protect price and profit margin, leaves you vulnerable to ruin by cheap price competitors, and makes being in business a misery, a fear-and-paranoia laden experience. If it is actually true that you must jump to answer your phone or cell phone or return calls or texts hastily, let it be a shrill, loud, clanging alarm bell, warning you that there is something profoundly amiss with your positioning, reputation, status, advertising, marketing, client selection, and other aspects of your business. They are in urgent need of attention.

In Atlantic City with my wife, I noted a long line behind us at Starbucks, where she wanted her morning coffee—a line made long by the near comatose state of the kid behind the counter they call a barista and the painful, slow-witted ordering of complicated drinks by customers who manage to reach the front of the line after a 20-minute wait still unsure of what they want. I also noted a walk-up pizza place directly across from the Starbucks serving coffee and pastries, with no line at all. She explained to me that Starbucks customers had been conditioned to wait patiently, expected to wait, and would wait, because it's Starbucks.

If Starbucks can pull this off with a true commodity—hot, brown water—you can certainly pull it off too. I can and do. So if you are dropping whatever you're doing and jumping every time your phone rings or buzzes as if stabbed in your rectum with a hot poker, be ashamed. Be very ashamed. And if you insist it's necessary, be scared. Be very scared.

Maybe this image will help: Picture the poor fellow walking around with cell phone in hand or on belt—or worse, with headphones on—as a big, dumb dog with collar and leash. Tug, tug, tug. Yap, yap, yap. Pant, pant, pant.

If you walk upright, you ought to behave better than this. And resent the leash.

Your "Steel Curtain" Telephone Defense

If you buy into the strategy of limiting and controlling access at all, you will obviously need a good screening system. What will protect you from the telephone? If you have a live person, a receptionist, or secretary, or a receptionist plus a secretary, that's probably best. (If not, you'll have to use voice mail.) Your receptionist or secretary may need a continually updated VIP LIST of people from whom you will take urgent incoming calls

You might wonder who's on my VIP List. I'll appease your curiosity. At any one given time, there are a dozen or so key private clients on that list—people paying me sizable sums of money. I have several friends. And that's it. I'd say that a VIP List with more than two dozen people on it is not a VIP List at all. In my case, even the VIPs can't get through to me immediately, because I'm not there, but they will get top priority for a pre-scheduled appointment call. On a given day, a client might be given a direct line to where I'm working, under extreme circumstances, but for one-time use only.

or be tracked down to return a call quickly. This prevents you from missing calls you really want, and it allows your assistant to screen all the other calls with great confidence.

Keeping this VIP List up-to-date helps prevent screening faux pas; however, even when a faux pas occurs, you must never sacrifice your assistant to the cause. You must support the person doing your screening 100% of the time. A screener can only do the job if she has complete confidence in what she's doing.

If you want staff to consistently put up a "Steel Curtain Defense" comparable in strength and reliability to the famous Pittsburgh Steelers' steel curtain defense of their glory years, you have to give them the right tools, equipment, and support.

You have to decide on the severity of the screening to be done. You will likely err toward liberal generosity, but should strive for tough-minded conservatism. This is about protecting your time and productivity. Every exception is a hole that weakens the entire defense system. Too many holes and you have a fortress constructed of thin-sliced Swiss cheese instead of thick, impenetrable brick.

On any given day, there may be several VIP calls and as many as a couple dozen other inbound calls—or faxes requesting access—from persons of uncertain priority. These may include existing clients without legitimate urgency, prospective clients yet to be screened and qualified, book reviewers, media contacts, salespeople, and peers. If I were in my office or accessible by cell phone and took these 27 calls as they occurred, and each lasted an average of only 3 minutes—and lots of luck with that!—I would have let loose of 81 minutes; 1 hour and 21 minutes. But much more importantly, I would be interrupted 27 times. The 3 minutes given each call would bear an added cost of 10, to get back in gear after each interruption. Now 13 minutes times 27 calls equals almost 6 HOURS OF LOST TIME. Further, some of those calls might actually be important but be handled half-assedly—if scheduled and dealt with as the priority of their assigned minutes instead of an irritating interruption, more might come from them.

We also employ screening with prospective new clients and some others. My assistant routinely requests a memo no longer than two pages, submitted by fax, describing the matter the person wants to discuss or the project he might wish my assistance with. I then have the flexibility of responding however I think best, which is often by fax rather than call because it is faster. A memo forces them to organize their thoughts, and it allows me to organize mine. Because these things accumulate and I tackle them at times of my choosing, as clumped work, one right after the other, I am in rhythm and can get through them much more quickly than with phone conversations.

At this point you will again be mumbling about all the reasons you can't do these sorts of things in your business because your business is different. Your clients won't tolerate it. You aren't this important. Pfui. It's not like I'm the President or the Pope or a Kardashian or anybody like that. I'm basically a self-glorified salesman. I've simply done three things anyone can do:

1. Decided.
2. Deliberately positioned and marketed myself in a manner conducive to controlling and limiting access.
3. Trained clientele. And they are trainable. When I was a kid, I had litter-box-trained pet rabbits that hopped back to their cage to go to the bathroom. I once had a racehorse trained to walk down the barn aisle and turn off the light switches with his mouth. If you can teach a bunny rabbit to go back to his cage to drop doody or a horse to flip light switches, you can train humans to respect you and your time and operate within a few simple rules.

You may or may not want to be as tough as I am. You may not even want to be as tough as many of my clients and many, many GKIC Insider's Circle Members in diverse businesses who've adopted modified versions of my approach. But I will bet you the biggest steak in Texas that you can benefit from a tougher screening process than you have now. Think about it.

Get a Grip on Email, Texts, and Faxes

Next, you've got to gain control over and productively use whatever communication tools and technology you permit yourself to use and permit others to use with you.

For me, that's only the fax machine—and for this I like it a lot. Unlike email, my faxes don't share space with massive clutter nor am I limited to a brief subject line nor do I worry much about instant deleting. From a receiving standpoint, it slows people down just enough to prevent thoughtless, sloppy, overly frequent communication, yet it is still instantly transmitted and received. If you want to use email, want to text, want to communicate and invite communication via Facebook or LinkedIn, and/or whatever new devil is birthed by the time you read this book, be my guest. They all have a dark side, although some are worse than others. It's critical to understand and manage the dark side.

The Dark Side of Instant Communication

Here's the problem. People who communicate with you instantly, if not also hastily and easily, have an expectation of immediate or at least quick response from you. Incredibly, they have this delusion that faxing a document or sending an email is the same as physically striding up to you and slamming it into your hands. There is an aura of immediacy to all of this that never existed with letters put in envelopes and handed over to the postal system or even to letters sent overnight by Federal Express. This has two evils. One, if the aura of immediacy is allowed to exist, you go through business life constantly disappointing people. It doesn't matter if their expectations are unreasonable; they are what they are. Two, you are under duress, tyrannized by this aura of immediacy.

This has been and occasionally still is a problem for me, just with fax. Were I to ever open the floodgate of email, I'd drown. You will too, if you don't get a grip.

With each easier, faster means of communicating, the quantity of dumb, junk communication has multiplied. Because sending an email is so easy and doesn't even require the labor of walking over to the fax machine, people send emails any time they have a brain fart. One consultant friend of mine was getting 8 to 20 different, separate emails each day from one of his clients—each time the client had a thought or question, zap went the email. In the corporate environment, the individual emails have become another Time Vampire trick, a less laborious equivalent of just popping in, standing in the doorway, saying, "Got just a minute?"

Finding Power in Communication Tools

What is the purpose of all this stuff—fax, email, texting, cell phone?

You may have fallen into the trap of thinking it's supposed to make access to you by others easier and faster and cheaper. Not so. You are to be concerned with you, not them. The only sane purpose is for this stuff to be used by you in a manner that improves your productivity and allows you to increase your income.

If you will train your clients or customers, associates and employees, vendors and others to communicate with you in thoughtful ways, by fax, or by email, no more frequently than some agreed upon number of times per day or week, with expectation of delayed response, that's a huge productivity advantage. It ends phone tag. Reduces your return call burden. Gets information to you in a more organized way. Lets you deal with these in-bounds at your pace, in the priority you assign, as you see fit.

I recommend at least prohibiting texts. These are the worst of hit 'n run communications. People send texts like "Kitchen caught fire. We're okay." Or "Billings Corporation deal has come apart. Discuss when you can." You come out of a meeting, arrive on the ground after a long flight, or are otherwise held back from seeing these and instantly responding in

Incidentally, if YOU want to communicate with me, you can fax me at 602-269-3113. Just don't sit there holding your breath, waiting for my response.

real time. You now get to worry and stew until you can get to the person. It is the electronic equal of the kids' Halloween trick: Pile dog shit on the stoop in front of the door, pin stuck in the doorbell, run. Watch the dummy yank open the door and step into the shit. And the pranksters are nowhere to be found.

Forcing faxes rather than email will also be more productive for you. I've looked at the emails people get and compared them to the faxes I get. More thought goes into the faxes. People tend to cluster multiple items into one fax vs. a stream of single-item emails. They are more inclined to resolve some things themselves when they must put them into a memo to be faxed than when they can email. The email is more casual, and you really don't want people feeling too casual about consuming your time.

Come to your own conclusions about it all—fax, email, text, cell phone. But be the master, not the slave.

Now, a special word about social media. Stay out of it altogether or impose strict discipline on yourself. It is amazing how much time disappears into YouTube watching and telling each other to go see things on YouTube. To Facebook etiquette, liking those who like you. Etc.

I'll tell you something you probably won't want to believe. I know a lot of rich, very rich, and very, very rich entrepreneurs. The richer they are, the less they personally have anything to do with any of this. They may have somebody creating the illusion of their participation, if they feel that aids their business' sales or their fame somehow. But they aren't looking at it or engaged in it, at all. And for the record, getting and being rich is behavioral. You can't seek the goal but opt for incongruent behavior different than that of those who achieve the goal, any more than you can claim sobriety but still get drunk every once in a while or claim to follow the Atkins diet except for eating bread.

This stuff is mindless entertainment for the masses. A means of feeling important for the chronically unimportant. Distraction from unsatisfactory real life. It is as potentially addictive as crack cocaine. It is damaging to your ability to concentrate. It is incredibly childish. The busy, success-oriented entrepreneur should have no time available for the digital water cooler conversation, the reporting of trivia, the rushing to be among the first 7 million to see a celebrity who forgot to put on her panties.

To be fair, social media, increasingly, can be useful in marketing, but that should be treated as media—not something you do. It's a subject for another place and time. It is a complicated subject. A survey by *DM News* of its readers, all direct marketing professionals, asked, "What is currently over-complicating your work life?" The top item: incorporating social media into marketing strategies and tactics. There is room for debate about its relative worth, the comparative quality of the customers it produces, how much time and attention it deserves, all situational to different kinds of businesses targeting different kinds of customers. But as something to be involved with personally, there's no legitimate debate. It's a time sinkhole that can be very hazardous to your wealth.

But if you must, as I said, strict discipline. Limit and track your number of permitted minutes per week, and when you hit the cap, stop, no matter what. Be careful of who you let in, who you like and follow, and the expectations you permit others to have about your participation. And whatever you do, do not "mouth off" in these places. Countless athletes, celebrities, politicians, corporate CEOs, and others have caused themselves immeasurable grief, negative PR to manage, unintended controversy to respond to—all a big, fat, costly time suck—by thoughtlessly and casually posting some comment or sending some tweet. Just during the months I was writing this book, instances have made national news of different CEOs and business owners running afoul of FDA, FTC, and SEC rules with single, casual tweets. It has recently been revealed that the

IRS freely examines anyone's email it chooses, after an arbitrary 180 limit. None of this is casual cocktail party conversation; it is broadcasting. None of this is private. There is legal, financial, and professional hazard *and* time suck.

You will be under ever mounting peer, friend, and other pressure to participate more and more in an ever-growing and expanding portfolio of these social media sites and services and activities. This is part of the world conspiracy to devalue your time and steal your productivity. Mostly idiots and fools, followers of the followers, not with evil intent, but nonetheless dangerous to you. They have a perfect right to their buy-in to all this, but you have a perfect right to your opt-out as well. I eat meat but rarely try to convince a devout vegan to join me in wolfing down prime rib, and I expect the vegans I know not to try and push their tofu and twigs on me. Same with this. Don't let yourself be intimidated. Make your own decisions for your reasons. Establish your own rules.

I am, by far, not the only one sounding alarms about the surrender of time and thought to technology-driven pressure. In fact, there's a growing chorus. One such voice belongs to Douglas Rushkoff. For the record, he is a young, tech-savvy man, not a grumpy old fogey.

In his provocative book *Present Shock: When Everything Happens Now,* he presents rich information and analytical thinking about four enemies I believe entrepreneurs need to be very aware of and guarded toward.

One was first warned of in a much older book, from 1970, Alvin Toffler's *Future Shock.* Toffler predicted a coming diminishment of everything that isn't happening right now and the onslaught of everything that supposedly is. He also warned we would be unprepared to manage the onslaught. Rushkoff writes of the tyranny and distraction of immediacy, robbing us of the ability to be thoughtful about anything, to benefit from perspective or context, and to follow a narrative begun some time ago and evolving over time. The chief danger of this to entrepreneurs is in impulsive, pressured decision-making with far too little information.

The Fed Chairman, as I write this, Benjamin Bernanke is ranked as one of the top experts on the history, makings, and recovery from The Great Depression, and he insists that you can't possibly make sense of the crash we experienced around 2008, that we are still trying to crawl out of, if you are ignorant of the Depression. Do we really want decisions made about an escalating conflict with North Korea today by people ignorant of the Cuban Missile Crisis or the Korean War? Most great business thinking and decision-making, even innovation, has a legacy. In my field of advertising, any copywriter working in a category, say "beauty," who thinks only of what is immediately occurring in front of him, and ignores the history and evolution of beauty product advertising and is ignorant of the greatest ads and advertising techniques in this category—like "Does She Or Doesn't She?" or "Rinse And Repeat"—is guilty of malpractice. The idea that everything happens now ignores that everything that happens now happens for reasons with roots.

Rushkoff's second caution is about what he calls *digiphrenia*— digitally induced mental chaos. You cannot be proactive and in control if you are incessantly reacting. For many, their boss is no longer the higher-up in the corner office or their client. It is the device in their pocket. Or devices, as men are warming to the idea of carrying man-purses because they have too many gadgets.

His third caution is what he calls *filter failure*. I often talk about this as democratization of sources and content. With instant access to more information on any subject than ever has come the problem of everybody's instant ability to create and distribute that information, and it is nearly impossible to discern the knowledgeable from the fools, the credible from the freshly imagined. He points to a single Facebook post having more impact than 30 years of scholarship on the same subject— because people are paying attention only to what is in their face at the immediate moment, regardless of source.

One of my roles, to readers of my five different business newsletters, and at a more exclusive level, to members of my mastermind group and to my private clients, is as a knowledgeable and trustworthy filter. I process over 200 trade journals, newsletters, and other business media and books every month. I am actively engaged with clients in diverse fields using every media, and, overall, a recipient of a monstrous amount of current information, opinion, and reportage of change. I discredit much of it, discard most of it, distill the best of it, and deliver it in a digestible form. But not only am I a filter, I also have, pay for, and rely on filters myself. Paid research from select sources is one of my most significant expenses. The old, traditional filters are all broken and, for many people, circumvented. Encyclopedia assembled by responsible editors assisted by buildings full of fact-checkers have been replaced by Wikipedia, an open media in which anybody can contribute, alter, and wildly fictionalize its supposed information. TV news broadcasts on three networks with responsible editors and producers demanding verified facts have been replaced by opinion broadcasts on a dozen network and cable channels and by easily and often manipulated online media and websites rife with opinion, rumor, gossip, and speculation. I recommend reading Ryan Holiday's book about this, *Trust Me: I'm Lying*. It is a brutally candid confession, chilling expose, and, for those interested in manipulating the media, a how-to guide. If you treat all information flowing to you as equal, if you fail to filter or have filtering done for you, then you are going to be more a victim than a beneficiary of the information explosion.

Finally, Rushkoff says, "I am less concerned with whatever it is that technology may be doing to people than what people are choosing to do to one another through technology. Facebook's reduction of people to predictively modeled profiles and investment banking's convolution of the marketplace into an algorithmic battleground were not the choices of machines." I would add that the thing to be most concerned about, over which you have the greatest possible control, is what you are permitting technology to do to you, by your own hand or by others.

Set the Timer on the Bomb

Almost 100% of my own phone calls occur by preset appointments, with start and end times. But if you do take an incoming call, when you get on the phone with someone, it's a smart idea to set up the exit time first. For example, I would say:

> *Tom, I have a conference call starting in just 15 minutes, but I wanted to take your call—I hope that will be enough time for our discussion. Do you agree—or should we set up another telephone appointment?*

Tick, tick, tick.

When someone "drops in," and you decide to go ahead and see them, then, when you bring them into your office, it's a smart idea to set up the exit time first.

> *Bob, it's difficult these days for me to see drop-in visitors, but it's good to see you. We'll only have half an hour, though, but no longer, as I have an important conference call set for 4:00 P.M. That's OK, isn't it?*

Tick, tick, tick.

You may not win any awards for being sociable, but you'll have shorter, more purposeful telephone conversations and meetings. Drop-ins will gradually get the message. Callers will gradually learn to call ahead and set up a phone appointment, or at least to prepare and be efficient when calling. I call this "setting the timer on the bomb." I even have a clock that looks just like six sticks of dynamite wired together, with a timer on it, and the timer has a flashing red light. This gets a lot of attention plunked down in the center of the conference table. If you're not going to do this physically, you at least want to do it verbally.

Most people will suck up about as much time as you let them. Salespeople feel productive and satisfied as long as they're talking with customers, and will even extend conversations with a friendly customer as a means of avoiding the risk of confronting new prospects. Employees will dawdle in conversation; it beats working! Conversations have a way of stretching to fill whatever amount of time is available for them.

Be Busy and Be Obvious About It

Obviously busy people are interrupted less than unbusy people. Just like burglars pass up some homes in favor of others, looking for the easiest, safest targets, those who steal and suck up time by interrupting others tend to cruise the office looking for the best opportunity and the easiest target. If you are sitting at your desk, appearing relaxed, you're it. Of course, you might be contemplating a formula for disarming a nuclear warhead, but that won't matter, because it's not obvious.

When you are visible to others, it's best to be visibly busy.

How Often Is the Average Worker Interrupted?

Every 3 minutes, 50 seconds. Overall, 44% of these are self-interruptions, and 56% inflicted by others, in person or via attention given to phone calls, texts, email, etc. That equates to 137 interruptions in an 8-hour work day. If you aspire to be only an average worker achieving average performance and average outcomes, then going along with this will meet your needs and guarantee your mediocrity.

This is actually a very simple premise: Attitudes and actions have direct consequences. If you accept the attitudes of the average—in this case, accepting frequent interruptions as unavoidable—and you accept the behavior of the average—in this case, the habit of distraction and self-interruption and of instantly, quickly, or even same-day response to interruptions inflicted by others, you can count on being and staying average. You cannot start drinking every morning, drink all day, consume a bottle or two of booze daily, and defend the behavior to yourself and others and expect to be anything other than an alcoholic. Similarly, you cannot accept and engage in any attitudes and behaviors of the mediocre and reasonably expect to be anything other than mediocre.

Statistics from: *The Book of Times* by Lesley Alderman

CHAPTER 4

The Number-One Most Powerful Personal Discipline in All the World

And How It Can Make You Successful Beyond Your Wildest Dreams

Shined shoes save lives.

— GENERAL NORMAN SCHWARZKOPF

I'm sure there are exceptions somewhere, but so far, in 35-plus years of taking note of this, everybody I've met and gotten to know who devoutly adheres to this discipline becomes exceptionally successful AND everybody I've met and gotten to know who ignores this discipline fails. Is it possible that this one discipline alone is so powerful it literally determines success or failure?

The discipline that I am talking about is *punctuality*. Being punctual. Being where you are supposed to be when you are supposed to be there, as promised, without exception, without excuse, every time, all the time. I cannot tell you how important I believe this is. But I'll tell you some of the reasons why I believe in its indescribably great importance.

First of all, being punctual gives you the right—the positioning—to expect and demand that others treat your time with utmost respect. You cannot reasonably hope to have others treat your time with respect if you show little or no respect for theirs. So, if you are not punctual, you have no leverage, no moral authority. But the punctual person gains that advantage over staff, associates, vendors, clients, everybody.

Dan Kennedy's #4 No B.S. Time Truth

Punctuality provides personal power.

The Tragic Case of the Doctor Who Couldn't Tell Time

Some years back, I had a client, a doctor of chiropractic, with a million-dollar-a-year practice and a rather large staff. It was particularly vexing to him that he was unable to rely on any of his staff members to be punctual. Some were habitually late getting to work on time. Others were habitually late getting back from lunch. Others habitually fell behind in getting important paperwork done. And so on. He tried everything—punishments and rewards—and nothing worked. Why? In all the years I knew him, I can't recall this doctor ever getting anywhere on time himself. He was even 20 minutes late one morning picking me up at my hotel so I could go and teach a time management seminar to his staff! Incredibly, my client never acknowledged the obvious problem here. Maybe there weren't any mirrors in his house.

The Telling Connection between
Punctuality and Integrity

It is my conviction that a person who cannot keep appointments on time, cannot keep scheduled commitments, or cannot stick to a schedule cannot be trusted in other ways either.

Fundamental dishonesty expresses itself in many different ways, but this is definitely one of them. I think it is significant that the man I consider to be the second most frequently and consistently dishonest and disreputable U.S. president of my lifetime, Bill Clinton—famous for his tortured deconstruction of the word "is"—was also notorious for being on "Clinton Time"—meaning anywhere from 20 minutes to two hours late to everything, thus being disrespectful to everyone.

There is a link between respect for others' time and respect for others' opinions, property, rights, agreements, and contracts. A person reveals a great deal about himself by his punctuality or lack of punctuality. So, as a general rule of thumb, I use this as a means of determining whether or not I want to do business with someone. And, when I violate this, as I occasionally foolishly do, I always get burned.

Let me give you one example. Back when I was still flying commercial, a person seeking to do business with me arranged to meet me at an airport, where I had a 90-minute layover. We agreed, and I confirmed by fax that we would meet at my arrival gate, at my arrival time, and then go to that airline's club room right there on the concourse for the meeting. When I arrived, the guy wasn't there. Some ten minutes later, I'm paged and told to meet him in the main terminal where he is because he ran late getting to the airport. It takes me ten minutes on the tram to get to the main terminal, and I have to cut another ten minutes of our meeting to allow time to get back to my gate. I have to go through this to meet with a man so disrespectful of a commitment made and of my time that he cannot organize his life to arrive at a meeting on time in his own home city. If he could not be relied on to honor such an easy commitment, why should anybody believe he would honor more important ones?

Still, violating my own rule, I went ahead and accepted this guy as a client. It was predictably ugly. He lied, he cheated, and he was completely disorganized, dysfunctional, and unreasonable. He sucked up a pretty good chunk of my time and cost me thousands of dollars to get rid of him. It's not the first time this scenario has taken place in my life. I suppose it won't be the last. But it IS a very reliable principle:

People who can't be punctual can't be trusted.

For ten years, I appeared 25 to 30 times each year on the number-one speaking tour in America, often addressing audiences of 10,000 to 25,000 people at each event. I was privileged to appear on these programs with many famous speakers, authors, politicians, entertainers, and business leaders, including Paul Harvey, Larry King, Coach Tom Landry, Coach Lou Holtz, former Presidents Bush #41 and Ford, Rev. Robert Schuller, "Cookie Queen" Debbi Fields, Olympians Mary Lou Retton and Bonnie Blair, speakers Zig Ziglar and Tom Hopkins, and the list goes on and on. As the last speaker on a long, full day's program, it was very important to me that the speaker ahead of me stuck to his allotted time and finished on time. It is the professional thing to do. It is respectful to the audience, respectful to the person hiring the speaker, and respectful to the speaker who follows. Most of these speakers understood this and performed accordingly. However, General Colin Powell, who I followed some 40 times, couldn't quite get it done for some reason, typically running 5 or 10 minutes long—but at least he graciously urged the audience to be sure and stay to hear me. Each year, I sent him a gag-gift clock of one kind or another as a Christmas gift and gentle reminder of "our" little problem.

One time, I spoke after then New York Governor Mario Cuomo at one of these events. He was an unbelievable time hog. He didn't just go 5 or 10 minutes beyond his 45-minute time—he went an unbelievable 20 minutes over! On stage, facing the governor, was a big, digital, red-lighted timer flashing 00:00 after his time ran out, flashing 00:00 for 20 minutes! He ignored it. Staff people signaled him from the side of the stage. He ignored them. I wouldn't trust him as far as I could throw him.

A Simple Way to Favorably Impress Others

Now, here's a "success secret" for you: I'm not the only person to have figured out this punctuality-integrity link. I'm just not *that* smart. I've stumbled on something that a whole lot of other smart, successful, and influential people already know and secretly use to make their determinations about who they will buy from or not buy from, do business with or not do business with, help or not help, trust or distrust. If you are not a punctual person, others you wish to positively influence negatively judge you.

If you think that successful people—people you want to deal with—do not have their own little "systems" for judging people, you're very naïve. Not only do they have such a system, most successful people make a point of having "instant reject criteria,"

Dan Kennedy's #5 No B.S. Time Truth

By all means, judge. But know that you too will be judged.

to save time in determining who they want to deal with and who they don't.

One of my most recent books, *No B.S. Guide to Trust-Based Marketing,* makes this point: Potential customers, clients, patients, investors, joint venture partners, and others have a short list of questions they are trying to answer in their own minds about you, and these questions typically take precedence over the merits of whatever proposition, product, or service you represent. The sophisticated salesperson, entrepreneur, or negotiator strives to answer these critical questions with demonstration rather than mere assertion. Often, that means by his personal behavior. Getting to yes with more of the people you attempt it with and getting to yes faster are both time-value/productivity and income improvement opportunities, so understanding these questions and effectively answering them by demonstration can have a very significant impact. For the full discussion of this, get a copy of *No B.S. Guide to Trust-Based Marketing.* But know that one of the demonstration behaviors that influence a great many people is punctuality.

One of my earliest business mentors said that there were only two good reasons for being late for a meeting with him: one, you're dead; two, you want to be.

So, to borrow from Dale Carnegie, if you want to win friends and influence people, be punctual.

And, if you'd like to save yourself a lot of time and trouble, start using this as a means of judging those who would do business with you.

Are Even a Person's Deepest, Darkest Psyche Secrets Revealed by Punctuality?

Punctuality even reveals a lot about an individual's self-esteem. We all know that kids who vandalize other people's property for sport, abuse their bodies with drugs, engage in promiscuous, casual, unprotected sex, and otherwise sabotage themselves are, in part, painfully demonstrating low self-esteem. They do not feel that they are important. Therefore, no one else and nothing else is very important, and anyone or anything that does seem important is deeply resented. I'd suggest that the adult who does not keep such simple commitments as appointments is not only saying to you that you and your time are unimportant but is unwittingly revealing that he does not feel he and his time are important either. He is, in essence, making a low self-esteem statement.

Some people with poor self-images and needy egos are deliberately late as a means of trying to be and seem important. Their intended message is: I can keep you waiting because I'm more important than you are. But the message they actually deliver, to those perceptive enough to read behind the lines, is: I don't have much self-respect, so I'm desperately trying to make myself feel more like a big shot by stealing your time and getting away with it. Pathetic. And a big, fat warning signal. Deal with this person and you are letting yourself in for all manner of abuse.

CHAPTER 5

The Magic Power that Makes
You Unstoppable

If you're going to do something tonight that you'll be sorry
for tomorrow morning, sleep late.

—COMEDIAN HENNY YOUNGMAN

If I'd known I was going to live this long, I would have taken
better care of myself.

—COMEDIAN PHIL HARRIS

O n the morning of my mother's funeral, I wrote
the following paragraph for the original, first edition of
this book:

*My mother passed away a couple of days, actually nights ago,
and the viewing was last night; the memorial service will be in
about four hours from now, this morning. It is 6:00 A.M. And
here I am, at the keyboard, in my home office, writing. That's
what I do almost every day, for at least the first early hour of
the morning, no matter what. And that's the answer to how I
can have five books in bookstores, a sixth and seventh hitting
early in 1996, be under contract for an eighth for 1997, write
my monthly newsletters, and so on.*

You can misinterpret, and I realize that. It's not that I'm devoid of emotion, nor that I did not love my mother. However, I learned long ago the vital importance of regimen, ritual, commitment, and discipline in relationship to successful achievement. So it takes a lot to derail me. Most people are much, much more easily distracted. Perhaps I'm extreme in my insistence on proceeding with my work plans no matter what, but most people are even more extreme in their willingness to set aside their work plans for just about anything—hangnail, stiff breeze.

How a "Little Man" Reminds Us of "The Magic Power" 8,000 Times and Counting

Some of you may know that I'm a horse racing aficionado. For me, a bad day at the track beats a good day at the office. I could relate when George Burns as God in the movie *Oh God!* headed off to the track with a racing form stuck in his back pocket to watch "the magnificent animals I created. I did very good work there." The racetrack is one of the most interesting places on earth. And there, like everywhere we really look, we can find powerful reminders of what it takes to excel in this world.

At age 46, Laffit Pincay, Jr., had accomplished just about everything a jockey can hope to accomplish. He had won the Kentucky Derby, The Belmont, six Breeder's Cups, the Eclipse Award five times, and he had already been in the Sports Hall of Fame—for 18 years. In 1995, he won his 8,000th race. He retired at age 56.

You wouldn't have found any racing authority who would have bet that Pincay would still be riding, winning, and winning more frequently than most, at the old-for-athletes age of 46, and on to 50. To a man, we would all have been against Pincay. It is one thing for a Nolan Ryan to have defied age in baseball. For an occasional top-performing player to defy age in football—at different times Jerry Rice, Brett Favre, Ray Lewis come to mind. But as a jockey, Pincay had to somehow keep his weight to 115 pounds. His frame would ordinarily have carried 140 and, with age, as we all seem to do, take on 10, 20, even 30 more pounds in that spare tire around the waist. But Pincay stayed at 115.

For most, the mental strain of this would prove impossible. Pincay probably learned more about nutrition, weight loss, and diet than anybody—because he had to. He had to know precisely how many calories and fat grams were in each bite of food he swallowed. When preparing his own meals, he had to measure each portion to the ounce. There was a book-length list of foods he could NEVER eat. To satisfy his taste buds, to fool his taste buds, he sometimes chewed on a piece of cake or other "sweet," but then spit it out like a wad of chewing tobacco. Every day, every meal, he had to exercise rigid self-control. At his age, if he slipped and gained a pound, he might never get rid of it.

Most days, Laffit Pincay put on a warm-up suit and speed-walked the track where he was racing, clockwise, at a time of day before he had to get ready to ride but as late in the morning as possible so as to take full advantage of the hot sun's ability to burn off any excess fluids in his body. He had a strict, demanding, daily exercise regimen. And ounce for ounce, inch for inch, he may have been the best conditioned athlete in America. Pincay's body fat percentage was, well, so near zero it wasn't worth measuring. He had the upper body of a weight lifter. His thigh muscles rivaled Schwarzenegger at his prime. A famous orthopedist involved in sports medicine described him as a perfect miniature replica of an NFL linebacker.

And let's remember that this "little fellow" climbed up on and controlled 1,000-pound beasts. If you watch

> $\mathcal{S}$elf-discipline is the magic power that makes you virtually unstoppable.

Thoroughbred horse racing, you'll quickly see that this is no easy task. Perched like a bird on top of an elephant, the jockey cannot control the horse through brute strength. There is that, but there is more. A horse either respects his jockey or he does not. Most respected Pincay. A 115-pound embodiment of extraordinary, applied self-discipline that commanded respect from beast as well as man.

How to Make the World Hand Over Just about Anything You Ask

Having and commanding the respect of others is a tremendous advantage in life. That edge comes from self-discipline. Having a (preferably private) sense of superiority over others is another power-producing edge. That, too, comes from self-discipline. The highly disciplined individual does not have to point a gun at anyone to take what he wants; people "sense" his power and cheerfully give him everything they've got.

Take a look at how little discipline most people have. I admit, I couldn't match Laffit Pincay. One of America's greatest humorous speakers, Charlie Jarvis, told of coming home from a trip and confessing to his wife that he'd violated his diet and wolfed down a Snickers bar at the airport snack shop. After she chided him, he pointed out that he had actually demonstrated enormous self-discipline: "I wanted to wolf down ALL the Snickers bars." I'm sorry to say, I was in that category more often than not for years. Still, compared to most of the people I observe, I was a self-discipline master even then. These days, I must control what I eat much more carefully than ever. I peeled off 45 pounds from my heaviest peak; I keep that off and my diabetes in check without prescription medication of any kind. I must pay attention to carb counts and blood sugar levels, and I take about 50 different vitamin, mineral, and herbal supplements a day. Compare that to the average "wide-load" American, who can't go a full day resisting junk food.

I have noticed since I took off my fat and got my physical condition under better control my income has gone up. Is this coincidental? Maybe. Complex? Maybe. But quite probably it reflects an unconscious preference on clients' part to have confidence in, to trust, to give money to, to meet the fee demands without question of someone who appears to have self-esteem, self-control, self-discipline. Food—pardon the word—for thought.

Take a look at how little self-discipline most people have. The thousands of business owners I work with tell me more than half their rank-and-file workers frequently show up late for work. Ask an employer of size and you'll hear how big the problems of tardiness and absenteeism are. People do not even have enough self-discipline to get up in the morning! It seems that the majority of today's workforce cannot be depended on to read, write, count, or to do anything on their own to improve their skills. (Which is why they are replaced by automation, relocation of jobs to foreign lands, and through every other means possible.) This, a rapidly accelerating trend, as the quality of the American workforce declines and its cost rises. The pressures and threatened pressures of Obamacare are fueling a whole new wave of automation. I have a client who has replaced over 1,000 retail location salespeople with vending machines, and the machines are outselling the humans.

In my business dealings, I find more than half the people cannot seem to get to appointments and meetings on time or keep preset telephone appointments. Clients miss prescheduled coaching appointments. Vendors miss deadlines as often as they make them.

Woody Allen once observed half of success seems to be showing up. Ed Foreman, a popular motivational speaker, very successful businessman, and, I think, the only man to be elected to Congress representing two different states at two different times, says you can be certain of rapid advancement in most business organizations if you'll just do three things:

1. Show up.
2. Show up on time.
3. Show up on time, ready to work. So few do.

Laffit Pincay, Jr., never failed to show up, show up on time, 110% ready to give each ride his very best effort.

In the entrepreneurial environment, it is much the same. There's a lot to be said just for showing up on time, ready to work. (Not hung over. Not exhausted. Not distracted.) The meeting of deadlines and commitments alone causes a person to stand out from the crowd like an alien space ship parked in an Iowa cornfield. The ability to get things done and done right the first time will magnetically attract incredible contacts, opportunities, and resources to you. All of this is a matter of self-discipline.

Dan Kennedy's #6 No B.S. Time Truth

Self-discipline is MAGNETIC.

And self-discipline aimed and applied at a particular thing, as I do to writing, as Pincay did to fitness, is quite literally a magic power. When you focus your self-discipline on a single purpose, like sunlight through a magnifying glass on a single object, look out! The whole world will scramble to get out of your way, hold the doors open for you, and salute as you walk by.

The Inextricable Link between Time Management and Self-Discipline

It takes tremendous self-discipline to productively allocate and invest time and to stick to your intentions. It's said that "the road to hell is paved with good intentions," and I believe it. Although some people find it hard to believe, I'm one of the laziest guys on the planet. There's no internal force that drives me to work. Every morning, I have a little fight with myself, and I have to force myself to haul it out of bed and into the office. And I could quite happily forget it all, go find a hammock on the beach, and sleep all day long.

I think this is a secret true of a lot of very successful people. I think they are secretly lazy and become exceptionally self-disciplined out of necessity.

Because the entrepreneur is his own boss and can do as he pleases with his time, it is very important to be self-disciplined. The entrepreneur with a loose, buddy-buddy, easily forgiving boss will never accomplish much. It is the entrepreneur with the tough task master as a boss who excels.

Three Steps to Successful Achievement

Successful achievement of most worthwhile objectives— including being an infinitely more productive entrepreneur who makes the most of his time—is rarely easy, but is often simple. In fact, it can be boiled down to three steps.

1. Awareness

As a result of reading this book, you will have a different concept of time, valuing of time, and how you must exercise control over your use and others' consumption of your time in order to have a reasonable chance of achieving your goals and tapping your full potential. You will have new awareness of how your time is used or abused, invested or squandered, organized and controlled or let flow about at random. As the first step to new achievement, there is always awareness of problems and failings, and of opportunities and successes.

2. Decision

All achievement follows deliberate decision, with extremely rare exceptions of accidental achievement, like tripping over an untied shoelace, falling face down on the pavement, and seeing a wrapped stack of lost $100.00 bills lying against the curb you wouldn't have noticed otherwise. Absent that kind of freak accident, achievement can only follow decision. As a result of your thinking provoked by this book, you can develop certain decisions.

3. Action

There are three kinds of action: starting things or implementation, follow-through, and completion. When you have a decision, you have to start doing things about it. For some people this is hard, but for many people in many situations, starting is relatively easy. The person who decides on a new diet may find it easy, even exhilarating to take a huge garbage bag and empty the refrigerator and pantry of all offending foods. It's follow-through that is usually the hard part. That's where tough-minded boss-of-self comes to bear. As I've noted elsewhere in this book, relying on sheer willpower is rarely successful. An environment has to be created in which high self-discipline is supported. But self-discipline is required. And rewarded.

"It is important that you get clear for yourself that your only access to impacting life is action. The world does not care what you intend, how committed you are, how you feel or what you think and certainly it has no interest in what you want and don't want. Take a look at life as it is lived and see for yourself that the world only moves for you when you act."

—Werner Erhard, Founder, EST

I would add that the world doesn't care how moral and righteous and justified or entitled you believe you are nor how immoral and unjustified others doing better at getting what they want than you are seem to you to be. Your opinions of yourself or of others or of justice itself do not matter.

My friend Robert Ringer, author of the classic *Winning Through Intimidation* (www.RobertRinger.com), says: Nothing happens until something moves. True, but further, hardly anything ever moves as you'd like it to unless you move it.

Even by random chance lottery winners must buy tickets.

"Success Leaves Clues"

It seems that the Creator thought it a good idea to leave clues to success all over the place, so that—if you have your eyes open— you can't stand in any one place, turn all the way around, and not find one. You can go to the racetrack, of all places, and find clues. You can watch spots on TV and find clues. You can pick up a magazine and find clues. You can drive down a street and look at the businesses and see clues.

The one thing that seems universal is that self-disciplined action is evident in every winner.

The great success educator Earl Nightingale once said that if you couldn't find a heroic, successful role model, just look at what everybody else is doing and don't do that. Look at how everybody else behaves, and do the opposite. It turns out that this is good advice for salespeople and businesspeople, but it would also be very good advice to kids stuck growing up in a ghetto or newly elected politicians in Washington.

When you look around at what I call The Mediocre Majority, you'll find that the one thing that appears universal with them is the lack of self-discipline.

CHAPTER 6

The Ten Time Management
Techniques Really
Worth Using

I'm going to graduate on time, no matter how long it takes.

—Senior Basketball Player, University of Pittsburgh

My business—*the information business, as well* as businesses such as weight loss, diet, and financial advisory services—revolves around the public's stubborn belief that there must be a "secret" to success, concealed from them, possibly by conspiracy, that if uncovered, would change everything. This concept can be useful to remember if you work in advertising, marketing, and selling, but it is a useless, even harmful, delusion otherwise. With regard to time, I promise you, there's no secret magic pill you don't know about. And no new, color-coded appointment book or iPhone app or super-duper gadget is going to change that.

In business, there are good strategies poorly executed, poor strategies executed well, but rarely is there a truly new, revolutionary strategy. In this chapter are ten good strategies. Nothing earth shaking, nothing revolutionary, probably nothing you don't already know. The issue is execution, not innovation.

The "joke" in the weight-loss industry, where I find myself doing marketing consulting from time to time, is this: If there were a diet that worked, there'd only be one diet. Similarly, you could reasonably argue that if there were one time management system that worked perfectly for everybody, there'd be only one system. The good news is that, in a way, there IS just one time management "system," and it's all here in this chapter.

If you read every time management book ever written, go to every time management seminar offered, and, more importantly, observe and analyze lots of people who get an exceptional quantity of important things accomplished, you will be able to boil ALL the technique "stuff" down to only ten things worth doing. So, let me save you all that time and just hand them to you here. I'll note, too, that all ten might not apply to you and your situations. When it's all said and done, you sort of have to find your own way.

Technique #1: Tame the Interruptions

As I discussed in detail elsewhere in this book, you've got to free yourself from the tyranny of the phone, text messages, email, faxes, and similar stuff. If you refuse to limit and control access to you, the war is lost even if you win a few battles here or there.

Technique #2: Minimize Meetings

Find every way possible to minimize your time spent in formal meetings. Most meetings end where they begin anyway.

I deal with one company that has six conference rooms—a very bad sign. If Noah had convened a meeting of architects, interior decorators, goat and sheep herders, lion tamers, navigators, we would all have fins. Nothing ever got done in a meeting. I hate 'em.

For a lot of people meetings are a place to hide out. Or preen and be important. But not a place to actually do work or get anything done. You need a strategy to avoid them. If you lead meetings, you need a strategy to abbreviate and focus them. If you must attend meetings, you need a strategy to escape from them at will.

*O*h, and here's a "little tip" that saves me quite a bit of time: Stop meeting people at restaurants for lunch or drinks, or whatever. Four out of five times, they'll keep you waiting. For years, when I spent time at an office, if I was going to lunch with somebody, I had them first come to my office, then we would go from there. Then, when they were 20 minutes late, I got to do 20 minutes of real work. If you must go to such an "off-site" meeting place, have something to read or some work to do with you.

Technique #3: Practice Absolute Punctuality

See Chapter 4.

Technique #4: Make and Use Lists   ·

There is not a single time management discipline or system on earth that doesn't revolve around making and using lists. You CANNOT carry it all in your head. For years, I've operated with four basic lists:

1. *My Schedule.* This is for the entire year, day by day.
2. *Things-to-Do List.* My basic "Things-to-Do" list is organized by the month, the week, and each day, prioritized as

A's, B's, and C's. Management consultant (and "hustler") Ivy Lee reportedly sold this idea to billionaire industrialist Andrew Carnegie's right-hand man, Charles Schwab, for $25,000.00. It worked for Schwab. It works for just about everybody who uses it now.

3. *People-to-Call List.* My third list is a "People-to-Call" list, also prioritized alphabetically.

4. *Conference Planner.* And finally, I have the "Conference Planner"—just a page for each person I interact with a lot, where I jot down things I need to talk to them about as they occur to me in between meetings or conversations.

To be perfectly honest, I do this with a yellow legal pad and pages I most often carry folded up in my pocket. And I'll admit that this is not exactly a shining example for a time management "leader" to set, but I've found that this works just as well for me as a number of different, more organized and formal systems I've tried. Over the years, I've experimented with the Day-Timer and several other systems, even one I designed myself. Anyway, the "magic" is more in the making and using the lists than in the particular tool, media, or format you use.

Incidentally, if you are a "free spirit," you might think something like these lists to be intolerably confining, like a pair of jockey shorts mistakenly bought one size too small. (What?—like I'm the only one to ever make that mistake.) Actually, once you get used to using these lists, you'll find them mentally, creatively liberating. Why? Because the more details you get on paper, the fewer you must remember and worry about remembering. This frees your mind up for more important tasks.

I also use a "storyboard" for planning, somewhat like the storyboard used to plan a TV program or movie. My speaking colleague Mike Vance, author of *Think Outside the Box*, teaches this method. As I've had Mike speak twice to my Insider's Circle Members in past years, quite a few of my GKIC Members and clients have learned this and use it, reporting great results.

I'm usually amused by people dependent on their devices and laptops for their schedules, plans, and lists. On more than one occasion, I've heard them wailing about the machine gleefully erasing everything and leaving them with a blank screen. Or watched their batteries go dead. So far, the tri-folded pages in my jacket pocket and pen have not failed me.

Ultimately, though, whether with crayon and pad or computer, you have got to get some sort of regimented, regularly used list-making system working for you. If you aren't making lists, you probably aren't making a lot of money either.

Technique #5: Fight to Link Everything to Your Goals
(The secret reason why there aren't more millionaires)

The late, great success philosopher Jim Rohn, a friend and speaking colleague, often said that the only real reason more people do not become millionaires is that they don't have enough reasons to. It's certainly not lack of opportunity! Look around. You can't pick up a magazine without reading of people who've taken very ordinary ideas, even weird ideas, and used then to become rich. You can't pick up a magazine and not read of someone who has scrambled up out of poor circumstances and gotten rich. So why don't more people become millionaires? They just don't have enough reasons to.

Similarly, I insist that the only real reason more people aren't much, much more productive is that they don't have enough reasons to. So, a secret to greater personal productivity is more good reasons to be more productive. That's why you have to fight to link everything you do (and choose not to do) to your goals.

Frankly, this is very difficult. You've undoubtedly heard the adage: When you're up to your neck in alligators, it's difficult to remember that your original objective was to drain the swamp. And, having been up to my neck in alligator-filled swamp water more often than I like to remember, I know just how tough it is to keep at least one eye fixed firmly on your list of goals. But that's EVERYTHING. That is what gets goals achieved. And that is what creates peak productivity, as I'll explain.

In the 1980s, "productivity" was a big, big buzzword. There were all sorts of folks running around teaching businesses and businesspeople every conceivable gimmick for improving productivity—without ever defining or (I contend) knowing what the heck productivity was. For corporations, there was regurgitated Demingism, Japanese management styles, MBO, MBV, and on and on. All in search of an invisible, ill-defined intangible.

If you're going to achieve peak personal productivity, you've got to *define* peak personal productivity.

Here's an old joke: The wife prevails upon her husband, an avid hunter, to take her along on the annual deer hunting trip, so she can finally see what all the fuss is about. To keep her out of harm's way, he stations her at the bottom of a hill and instructs her to shoot her gun into the air as a signal if she spots deer. Then he and the other guys head off through the woods, toward the creek, where deer are likely to be found. About ten minutes later, they hear not one but four quick shots. They race back to the hill, where the wife is standing, pointing her rifle at a fellow standing next to a fallen, dead horse. The guy is saying, "OK lady, it's your deer. But at least let me get my saddle."

If you don't know what peak personal productivity looks like, how are you gonna hit it?

So, here's my definition:

> Productivity is the deliberate, strategic investment of your time, talent, intelligence, energy, resources, and opportunities in a manner calculated to move you measurably closer to meaningful goals.

Note that this definition presupposes the existence of meaningful goals. I don't know of a single successful individual, in any field, who isn't goal-directed, and who is not involved in measuring, preferably daily, movement toward those goals. Paul Meyer, founder of Success Motivation Institute, once stated that if you are not achieving what you feel you should in life, it is because your goals are not defined well enough. But my definition of productivity goes beyond that. It says that you cannot be productive without goals, in fact, without linkage with goals. It says you cannot be productive without *measurement*.

This gives you a very simple standard for determining, minute by minute, task by task, choice by choice, whether you are being productive or unproductive:

> *Is what I am doing, this minute, moving me*
> *measurably closer to my goals?*

Now, to be reasonable, and to be human, let's cheerfully acknowledge that nobody can—or should—be able to say "yes" to that question all of the time. We need, want, and deserve time for casual conversation, for baseball scores, for political arguments, for reading the comics, for just plain goofing off. But you want to do those things knowingly, consciously, by choice, not by random accident or others' direction.

I'd say that anything beyond a 50% "yes rate" qualifies as peak personal productivity. Incidentally, measurement alone will enhance your productivity. Just asking the question will enhance your productivity. Any athlete will tell you that measurement alone improves performance.

Technique #6: Tickle the Memory with Tickler Files

I've got a memory like a steel trap. A rusted steel trap. Seems a lot seeps out through those rust holes. For example, I seem to have mental blocks about how old people are (the ONLY person's age I know is mine), birthdays, anniversaries, holidays, people's names. With this in mind, I wrote a country-western song: *I Love My Wife But I Can't Remember Where I Live*. Perversely, I can perfectly recall the lyrics from 20-year-old songs, obscure actors' names, and a collection of other useless trivia. If I could remember to phrase it as a question, I'd go on *Jeopardy!* and get rich. Seriously, I need tools and systems to substitute for memory. The Tickler File is one of my favorites.

The more I use this technique, the better I like it. The idea is simple: You have 90 file folders: red numbered 1 through 30; blue numbered 1 through 30; and white numbered 1 through 30 representing the current month, next month, and the month after that. This is most commonly used by accountant-type folks, to keep track of bills to be paid. But it can be used for anything. Let's assume you agree to follow up with a client on a particular matter on the 10th of next month. Take either that client's whole file or just that piece of correspondence or just a handwritten note and plop it into the Blue file folder numbered 10. And forget it. On the 10th of next month, it'll pop up all by itself and remind you to do it. Used right, these Tickler Files reduce clutter, serve as automatic memory, and help organize daily activities.

Yes, I am well aware that there are all sorts of "contact management programs" for computers, pads, and phones that can substitute for the file folders in a drawer, and if you prefer that, by all means, be my guest. (I have more to say about technology later in this chapter.) Personally, I'd be scanning in stuff, requiring time, and I'd have a hard time accommodating the lumpy and bulky material that is part and parcel of my work. But manual, automated, physical, virtual, or hybrid, a Tickler File System can be a very good friend.

Technique #7: Block Your Time

Here is one of the real, hidden secrets of people who consistently achieve peak productivity: Make inviolate appointments with yourself. You know, we all do a pretty good job at keeping the appointments we make with others. We have this skill down. So, why not use it to get things done?

Most people's schedules only have their locked-in-stone appointments with others. Mine also has my pre-allocated, locked-in-stone appointments with myself and with my work, with start and end times. For each year, a lot of time gets locked down months to a full year ahead. For example, I clump most of my necessary phone appointments during a month into one day, along with the group coaching calls I conduct, and the random teleseminars, radio interviews, and discussions with clients that pop up. While many of these things can't be known specifically six months ahead, I can and do book my Phone Day in each month a year ahead, then all needed calls are put on those days. Speaking engagements and coaching meetings are booked way ahead. Then month to month, the various work appointments: the time blocks for writing my monthly newsletters, for work on a book. My goal is to have as little unassigned time as possible. The less open and flexible time, the less wandering and meandering, the less waste, and the more discriminating in saying yes to things you have to do.

I treat the work appointments (or play appointments) I have with myself just as inviolate as I do a speaking engagement or a consulting day.

In short, if you lay your calendar out before you and pre-assign or block as much of your time as possible, as much in advance as possible— carved in rock not written lightly in pencil—you will then leave yourself only a small amount of loose, unassigned time. Further, by blocking time for important, high-value functions you perform, you

> S ome years back, I was counseling a chiropractor new to practice and advised her to close her office for one day a week, call that "Marketing Day," and devote that entire day to calling patients, visiting health food stores, calling on businesses, giving speeches, and so on. Left to be "fit in" as time allowed, most of these very productive things would never have happened.

prevent demands of others from moving your highest and best-value activities from number one to number ten on your list, over and over again.

When to Work. Or Workout. Or Whatever

As men age, their testosterone declines, and their peak testosterone is early in the morning—a fact that many wives are unenthused about.

It may well be that your body has its own clock for everything, not just sex. There's a growing body of research supporting the idea that your body and your mind are best equipped to most effectively perform different tasks. For example, exercising first thing in the morning may waste the time when you are mentally fresh and best able to do your most important work. Late in the afternoon, when the mind is fatigued and waning in cognitive function, could be the better time to hit the gym.

For more on this, see Sue Shellenbarger's book *The Peak Time for Everything*.

On the other hand, I believe you can train and condition your mind to your schedule.

I, for example, have trained my subconscious mind to solve assigned problems and to write advertising copy or content copy for me while I sleep. Scoff, but virtually every morning, at 6:00 or 7:00 A.M., I go directly from bed to computer, put fingers on keyboard, and race, race, race to input all the copy pouring from my subconscious, which has accumulated during the night and has been impatiently waiting to get it committed to the printed word. It feels somewhat like having waited way too long to pee, rushing to the bathroom, and barely getting your clothing out of harm's way before explosively powered urine floods the bowl—not that I'm comparing my writing to pee. Others make that comparison, and I'll leave them to it. But now, when I have to write, I have to write!

I am an Amazon shareholder and my books are sold by Amazon, but I have never once gone to Amazon and bought a book there. I can more quickly jot a book I hear or read about and want on a list or scrap of paper for my assistant to fetch. On the other hand, I will still go to a bookstore and meander about, looking at new titles, types of books I would not ordinarily be exposed to, or at the newsstand. It is an inefficient but effective method of discovery and a relaxing entertainment. So for me a two-fer, the same hour is productive in two ways.

This is an example of know thyself. The more you know about yourself and what works best for you, to liberate your creativity, to power your performance, the better you can arrange things to your satisfaction.

As another example, for the past 10 years, I've rarely had an assistant in my own work environment, and when I've tried it, I've found it disruptive and unproductive. That person actually takes over my time—the exact opposite of my reasons for employing her. There must be work organized for her to do when she arrives. Her questions must be answered. She requires supervision.

Instead, my assistant has been in her own office at the opposite end of the country. We speak briefly no more than once a day—for which we both accumulate, organize, and prioritize what must be covered. I put together her work at my pace and convenience and deliver it by FedEx once to three times a week. She organizes all my in-bound mail, faxes, phone messages, periodicals, plus her work and sends it each Friday. We do not email or text because I never use either one. We are both safeguarded from interruptions by the other. Neither of us wastes the other's time. Clients, vendors, and others learn that we are not in the same space and that she does not have immediate access, so she is able to ward off pressure to "just get him for me for a quick conversation now."

I recognize full well most people would not want this sort of arrangement even if proven to be the most productive of all approaches to having a personal assistant. Many bosses get psychic satisfaction from buzzing a buzzer, literally or figuratively, and having their assistant drop whatever he or she is doing and appear in front of him, panting and eager. This is food for their ego. Many like the social interaction of staff. I doubt many really need it, but many want it. It's far beyond the scope of this book to deal with psychosis. I am simply explaining to you that I have figured out how I am most productive and completely ignored convention in order to create the best work conditions for myself. It is those two things that are important:

One, to figure out how *you* are most productive.
Two, to throw out all norms, "rules," preconceived ideas, others' opinions, others' schedules, etc., and create the best

work conditions for yourself, those that facilitate your best productivity.

Understand this is the polar opposite of the trap most fall into. Most try to improve their productivity and manage their time inside boxes already built by others.

Technique #8: Minimize Unplanned Activity

By reducing unscheduled time and unplanned activity, you automatically reduce waste.

If you look around carefully, you'll see that most people just sort of show up. They arrive at the office and react. If you press them for their day's plan, you'll find they may have only one or two scheduled activities—one of which is usually lunch. (That attitude reminds me of the *Peanuts* cartoon: What class do you like best? Recess.) They may also have a few things on a "loose" things-to-do list. All the unscheduled time somehow gets used up, but if you again press them at the end of the day, or better yet, at the end of the week, they cannot tell you where it went.

Just as the person who cannot tell you where his money goes is forever destined to be poor, the person who cannot tell you where his time goes is forever destined to be unproductive. And, often, poor.

Ideally, you should schedule your day by the half-hour, from beginning to end. I now use the term "script" in place of "schedule." Many days, *every minute* is accounted for in advance and outcomes are pre-ordained.

If you do project work as I do, it's important to estimate the minutes or hours required and work against the clock, against deadlines. Every task gets completed faster and more efficiently when you have determined in advance how long it should take and set a time for its completion. This, too, minimizes unplanned activity.

Doesn't All This Create a Pressure Cooker Environment?

When you play "beat the clock" on a daily basis, with virtually every activity, from a phone conversation to writing a sales letter or answering in-bounds booked as appointments, with start and end times, you *do* create pressure for yourself. But once you grow accustomed to it, you'll discover an important difference between pressure and stress. Chaos, juggling priorities, randomly responding to interruptions, letting work expand its consumption of time as it sees fit, and constant compromise of your intentions to accommodate others, leaving many intentions unmet and carrying over endlessly creates a lot of pressure. Being organized as described in Techniques #7 and #8 creates pressure but actually reduces stress.

Pressure to Perform Can Make Performance Better

This may be contrary to what you've been told by others, but I know it to be true. Focus is everything, and nothing forces focus better than intense time pressure. One of the things I do is drive professionally in harness races, about 200 times a year. A race is 2 minutes or less, the difference between first and fifth place often just a fifth of a second. There are eight or nine other horses and sulkies in tight quarters, the width of a piece of paper separating the wheels. There is zero time to think about any of the three or four critical decisions and myriad of small ones that must be made during the course of the race. And being distracted can get you and others killed. The pressure is intense, so the focus is nearly perfect. The mind does not wander.

The co-host of Discovery Channel's show *Myth-Busters*, Adam Savage, is a movie special effects fabricator. He told this story in *Wired* magazine (2–13):

"I'm working on an alien costume. I've got the suit. It was built for me and it's gorgeous. But I'm making the head myself, and it's kicking my butt. The problem: I have too much time.

I've learned over decades of building that a deadline is a potent tool for problem solving. This is counterintuitive, because complaining about deadlines is a near universal pastime. . . . When I'm stumped without a deadline, I tend to let things go. So the head has pretty much sat on my bench for seven months. Any cursory perusal of a fan/maker forum on the web reveals two distinct kinds of projects: the long, meandering, inconsistently updated but impressively detailed effort, and the hell-bent for leather, tearing toward a deadline build. Solutions to problems of the first type are often methodical and obvious. Solutions for the second type are much more likely to be innovative, elegant, and shockingly simple. Invariably, the second type of project is propelled by an upcoming event. **Deadlines refine the mind.** They remove variables like exotic materials and processes that take too long."

His experience with his work is much the same as mine is with mine—writing advertising and sales copy for complex, multimedia campaigns and writing content for books, info-products, newsletters, and seminars.

Walt Disney and Steve Jobs were both notorious for placing "impossible" deadlines on projects and the people who worried over them and worked on them—and look how their ventures turned out.

There is a popular idea that one should escape and avoid pressure. I believe the opposite. I believe the more pressure you put yourself under to perform, the better you perform—and the less time each performed task or accomplishment requires, giving you time to tackle another and another and another. Both your conscious and subconscious minds are capable of much more than you now ask of them, and they and you can be conditioned to thrive under intense deadline pressure.

It Can't Take More Time Than This: The Power of a Time Budget

Certain pieces of business have certain relatively or perfectly predictable value for me. Not all entrepreneurs have as clear-cut a basis for making these determinations as I do, but everybody can develop some basis. In my case, for example, I know what a book like this can be worth to me in total income, from the royalties from the publisher, and from promotional considerations. There is a dollar number. I take that number, divide it by $2,000.00, and that dictates the maximum number of hours I can invest in writing this book, getting it through editing, corresponding with the publisher and others about it, and promoting it. It will get not a minute more. I know how much I will earn from a particular seminar. The hours required to travel to it and present it times $2,000.00 equal an amount deducted from the total. The remainder divided by $2,000.00 dictates how many hours can be invested in its promotion and preparation. It cannot have more. It does not deserve more. I could take you through virtually every piece of business within my entire realm of business activity and conduct the same math exercise.

This creates a time budget for each piece of business, project, client relationship, etc., that has to be binding. If I can see that something will require or even risks requiring more time than it is worth, I pass on it. If I am running out of time, compromises must be made in order to finish within the time budget. In most of what I do, you can tinker and tweak and try to improve endlessly. In my book *No B.S. Guide to Ruthless*

Management of People and Profits, I talk at some length about the GE-SPOT: the Good Enough Spot. Different businesses, different customers, different products all have GE Spots. In most cases, there is insufficient value in exceeding the GE Spot, but many entrepreneurs get caught up in far exceeding the worth of a piece of business by striving for perfection beyond the GE-Spot. I work against the clock, within the time budget, and to but never beyond the GE-Spot. I can frankly tolerate some compromise of desired quality, but I *cannot* tolerate winding up underpaid.

Very few people think this way. They make open-ended commitments, and work at things for as long as it takes to complete them. This is self-abuse. It guarantees you will invest too much time in relationship to the financial worth, because work expands to fit the time available to it.

Very few people develop time budgets, and even fewer engineer their work backwards based on those budgets. If I know the maximum number of hours that can be invested in this book's writing, I know the maximum number of minutes that can be invested in each page. I know page by page if I'm on pace, falling behind, or getting ahead. It's cool to get ahead. That banks time that, later, I can invest in more polishing than I'd planned on, or transfer to a different aspect of the piece of business like promotion, or pocket as bonus profit. It's bad to fall behind. Falling behind sets up the worst-case scenario: being underpaid for this piece of business and having to steal time from another piece of business. That's why falling behind has to be watched out for and fixed.

Technique #9: Profit from "Odd-Lot" Time

Everything is now portable. A seminar by a great speaker, just about any and every book ever published, how-to information of every variety, on audio CDs and DVDs, accessible through online media, inside your Kindle or Nook or iPad. Or you can still make sure you have an actual book with you at all times. You can use YouTube for something other than watching kittens water ski. There is no excuse to simply waste time while waiting in an airport, stuck in traffic, parked in a reception room. In Washington DC, they say a billion here, 10 billion there, before you know it you've spent real money. Well, 5 minutes here, 15 minutes there, pretty soon you're spending months.

The audio program is the greatest educational invention since the Gutenberg press—and has the superiority of not requiring exclusive attention to be beneficial. I've been producing and educating others for 40 years as well as educating myself with audio programs for 50 years, starting with records, then audio cassette tapes, now CDs. You can turn your car into a classroom. You can listen and think and absorb while doing mundane, relatively mindless tasks you either can't escape or don't want to. Some people *like* mowing their lawns. You can condition your subconscious with spaced repetition learning most easily with audio; 7 to 21 repetitions of the same messages automatically imbeds. Few will read the same book seven times.

Some people, instead, give their odd-lot time to returning calls, texts, or emails or to talking on the phone. This is usually a mistake for three reasons. One, you'll be doing it hurriedly and without proper preparation or organization, and if any of it is important, it's too important to do poorly. If it's not important enough to do properly, why are you doing it at all? Two, it's a bad precedent to set with those who have access to you and with whom you communicate. If you inject randomness, you lose the ability to impose organization. Three, it steals time you need to think, to read, to listen, to get and process input. Constant connectivity makes Jack a dull boy, dull meant as synonym for stupid.

Disciplined use of the time everybody else wastes can give you an edge. The now rich and famous writer of legal thrillers,

Scott Turow, wrote his first novel using only his morning commutes into New York City on the train. All around him, others just killed the same time. If I have big gaps between races I'm driving in, I take a stack of trade journals to skim or accumulated "B-pile" mail to go through, sit in the car outside the barn, and make an hour serve a productive purpose.

For most people, these minutes don't matter. But they can. In a sense, this is the penny argument. It's *only* a penny. A lot of people won't even pick one up if they drop it. But if you ask Warren Buffett or Donald Trump if they pay attention to pennies, you'll get a different answer. So when you say to yourself "it's only 10 minutes," you miss the entire point of time.

Technique #10: Live Off Peak

Why make life more difficult than it already is?

There are obvious ways to use this technique. For example, avoid going to the bank on Fridays, especially after 11:00 A.M., and especially if it is the 1st or 15th of the month. Avoid going to the supermarket the day before a holiday weekend. Avoid going to the post office the day before a rate increase (an unfortunately increasingly common occurrence).

I suppose everybody knows these things. But there are many similar patterns and instances of "herd behavior" that you can avoid. In Phoenix, where I lived for 24 years, I could drive from my home to my office in ten minutes if I did it after 9:00 A.M., but it took a half hour or more if I tried it between 7:30 and 8:30 A.M. Thanks to the idiotic refusal by the Phoenix authorities to install left-turn arrows, it was often easier, faster, and safer to make three right turns and go around a block than to wait in line and make one left turn.

If traveling, I try to avoid having to check out and leave a hotel between 8:00 and 9:00 A.M. or checking in between 4:00

and 6:00 P.M., because that's when everybody else checks in and out. When you take note of these things and organize your life to work around them, you can save a lot of time and avoid a lot of frustration.

Bonus Technique #11: Use Technology *Profitably*

I first wrote this book in 1996. It was updated once, in 2004. Now, once more. Even since 2004, the quantity and diversity of business and personal technology has mushroomed wildly.

There are so many tech tools to choose from, it's hard to make good choices.

Specific things people called my attention to as I was writing this include Dataminr, a software program that can purportedly process and screen as many as 400 million tweets a day in real time, extracting and distilling what you've told it is relevant to you, and delivering only that pertinent information to you via email and desktop alerts (www.dataminr.com). Makes me think of the computer system Batman created in *The Dark Knight* to eavesdrop on every phone conversation occurring in Gotham City, searching for keywords spoken. Expensify is, I'm told, a free app that links to your chosen credit card and automatically marks dates of purchases and categorizes them in an expense report for tax purposes or to submit to employer or client (www. expensify.com).

There is an almost infinite, endlessly multiplying array of these kinds of things, to manage just about everything for you. On one level, I'm amused by much of this. We are busily inventing new and often complicated tools to manage the complicated tools that are managing the complicated tools of our lives—and, ultimately, how many gadgets, tools, and apps can you manage before they take all your time? I am absolutely convinced that over-reliance on these things is weakening people's ability to think, reason, remember, much the same as a healthy person who chooses to be pushed about in a wheelchair everywhere will find his leg muscles atrophy.

Few reading this book will share my personal view. Most of the tech gadgetry is an anathema to me. That does not prohibit me having it used for me or having it deployed for me or my clients as advertising, marketing and sales media. It hasn't even barred me from investing in technology companies. I also own tobacco stock but have never smoked. Nor should my personal preferences be the advice I dispense. Instead, I have three cautions:

> **One, ask the tough question: Where's the profit in this?** If it does, in fact, honestly, conserve and improve the value of your time, aid you in faster or surer implementation, or otherwise boost your or your business's performance, then, of course, use it. But be very careful to consider its direct cost, i.e., the time required to use it as well as the indirect cost, i.e., what relying on it is doing to your brain.
> **Two, beware using something just because it exists**. The piling on of things to use and do because somebody invents and markets them puts you on the wrong side of the cash register. Kohler is selling a very pricey toilet/ bidet with a touch screen pad attached to "manage it." But, really, is there any practical benefit to a computer-operated toilet?
> **Three, beware peer pressure.** You are an adult entrepreneur. Don't act like a kid in junior high. Just because "everybody" around you has rushed to get the latest tech thing or stuff does not mean it is productive and profitable for you to have it—and the fact that "everybody" has embraced it should even give you pause. What's popular, what's normal, and what's productive often do not match up.

Automate or Stagnate

Automation can certainly facilitate implementation that would not be possible or would be considerably less profitable otherwise. My friends who invented Infusionsoft brought something forward that is a terrific example of this. If you read my book *No B.S. Guide to Direct Marketing for NON-Direct Marketing Businesses*, you'll be introduced to lead generation in place of one-step selling, multimedia, multistep marketing campaigns, and multistep follow-up campaigns for unconverted leads, new buyers' retention and ascension, and cross-selling. If all that was gibberish to you, please, please, please, do yourself the very profitable favors of getting and reading the book, and accepting the free offer on page 187.

Anyway, all this comes from big direct marketing companies with big computer systems filled with custom software they had built for them and teams of employees buzzing about managing it all. The small-business owner or entrepreneur has none of that and can't afford it. For years, we all did the best we could, doing all this manually, and, as computers came to every office and kitchen table, with various types of programs that didn't communicate well with each other. Most could, candidly, only implement everything I taught and they understood represented great opportunity to a very limited extent, with a relatively high quotient of struggle and pain.

Infusionsoft is the only small-business marketing management software built from the ground up to properly, easily run complicated, multistep campaigns. It combines database and list segmentation functions, CRM functions, tracking, automated email, and many other capabilities. I encourage looking into it, at www.infusionsoft.com. Most of my clients and many GKIC Members power their marketing with Infusionsoft, including many sophisticated campaigns that they can set up and forget, and know they'll occur perfectly.

As an example, for one group of entrepreneurs who sell by bringing prospective clients into introductory seminars and there scheduling personal, follow-up appointments with as many as they can but always a minority of those in attendance, I devised a 16-step, 4-week follow-up system for those not scheduling that produces from a 2-to-1 to 8-to-1 return on investment. Hardly any of these busy entrepreneurs would ever consistently implement it without Infusionsoft. Now, they only need enter or database migrate the people from the seminars not booking appointments and those prospects automatically get 12 email and 4 direct-mail follow-up communications, all customized and personalized, with precise timing (i.e., Follow-Up #1, 3rd Day, Follow-Up #2, 5th Day, etc.). Most businesses can be revolutionized with this kind of automated, no-fail follow-up.

So, make no mistake, I am for automation where it provides a clear advantage.

Sales and marketing is an area where automation reigns supreme, and every entrepreneur worth his salt will be constantly looking at these opportunities. My client, Guthy-Renker Corporation, has, over the past several years, replaced most of its human-staffed sales carts for Pro-Activ® in malls all across America with super sophisticated vending machines featuring video and touch screen ordering. Another client of mine, H.U.M.A.N./Healthy Vend, uses similar advanced technology machines. Fully automated webinars, with online registration, instant, automated confirmations, time-triggered multimedia follow-up, the playing of the webinar, order-taking, credit card processing, direct funds deposit, multistep follow-up to the nonbuyers—this is all now a part of the ecommerce landscape, and something for which I create a lot of sales strategy and sales copy, for countless clients. We began automating sales functions quite some years ago with "free recorded messages," and still use that tactic and device today.

Management is a place where technology can be immensely valuable. In my book *No B.S. Ruthless Management of People and Profits*, I champion the use of live-time and recorded video and audio surveillance of all employees and places within a business possible, especially those where scripted interaction with customers is supposed to occur. Owners in a wide variety of businesses including chiropractic clinics and dental offices, suntan salons, restaurants, retail stores, and others who have—in most cases, nervously—followed my advice on this unanimously report significant improvements in revenue and in staff compliance and productivity.

Personal performance can also be enhanced with both technology and automation, as already discussed. One of the most interesting sites in this category to check out is www. IdealMe.com, a "personal development technology" company I am advising and in which I am invested.

All of it, though, needs to be added to your business life carefully. It's best if what gets added replaces more time-consuming or cumbersome things that can be subtracted. Trying to give attention to more and more and more added with no subtraction gets problematic in a hurry.

A Few Words about Social Media

Rick Goings, the brilliant CEO of Tupperware, calls it "anti-social media." There is certainly that element: a divorcing from reality and from real communication. If it's important, a one-hour face-to-face meeting can be a lot more productive than a series of minute-length emails or tweets back 'n forth, back 'n forth. There is also a serious consumption of time that is not noticed or felt in the same way that talking with the same people in person or by phone for the same amount of time is noticed and felt. It can steal your time in little nips.

For the entrepreneur, there is the issue of using social media as an advertising, marketing, sales, and customer relationship media, and, separately, there is the issue of using it personally. The first requires a very long discussion, well beyond the parameters of this book, but I do not want to be misread as opposed to social media for such purposes. I have clients with very robust Facebook, Twitter, LinkedIn, YouTube, and other marketing efforts that they are able to track and hold accountable. These same clients, incidentally, are also heavy users of direct-mail, print, and broadcast media. My friend Perry Marshall has written an outstanding book about Facebook advertising, *Ultimate Guide to Facebook Advertising: How to Access 600-Million Customers in 10 Minutes.* But here we'll just talk briefly about personal use.

A 2013 survey of readers of *DM-News,* a trade journal of the direct marketing industry, collected reports from busy executives, copywriters, producers, and others. They said that the biggest increase in time spent in their lives is, drum roll please, using social media personally. For biggest time waster: answering emails. As an entrepreneur you really *need* to make a strategic decision about just how much unimportant communication, whether within social media or via incessant email carrying expectation of response, you are going to permit or permit occurring in your workplace during work hours. I have a friend I have dinner with two to three Friday nights a month. We have some business involvement and are good friends. We catch up during that dinner, time we find enjoyable. We do not tweet, email, check each others' Facebook sites, or chat 20 or 200 times during the week. I now find most people doing exactly the opposite. Nothing is walled off or boxed in. They are so frequently communicating in little blips and snippets, going to check in and update, looking, posting, etc., for *personal* purposes (not marketing held accountable by ROI), they are not functional entrepreneurs.

I know there is tremendous peer and friend/family pressure to actively participate in all of this, and more and more of it. But their agenda is quite different than yours should be. Their chief concern is not the safeguarding and best investment of your time, ability, and energy. I also know there is the pressure of the general idea that "everybody is on Facebook." But that ignores the large number who exit it every month, and the larger number who have static presence and no active involvement personally, or those who have it used only for business purposes with it delegated to others (as in my case). Sorry to burst your bubble, but "everybody" is not enthralled with it or Twitter, etc. And it certainly seems to me that the more successful the entrepreneur is, the less involved he is.

If you happen to have a home office and are able to work productively at home, you have adopted certain "rules" for yourself and for your family to separate your personal time and life from your work time and life. If "personal" is permitted to bleed over easily and randomly, work performance disintegrates. Social media is a bleeding over of all things personal—and often trivial—into your work time and life.

What Is the Average Length of Time People Spend Waiting in Line?

Sweden	2.2 minutes
U.K.	3.3 minutes
Italy	14.4 minutes
Russia	27.1 minutes
United States	16 minutes
@ Disney World	48 minutes
To be first to get newest iPhone	5.3 hours
U.S. Emergency Room	4.7 hours

Time People Spend Waiting in Line?, continued

Data from: *The Book of Times* by Lesley Alderman. Disney Guidebook: *Little-Known Facts about Well-Known Places at Walt Disney World* by Laurie Flannery; *The Unofficial Guide to Walt Disney World 2013* by Shelinger/Testa; *Time Use Survey,* Grey Research Group.

There are three possible attitudes to have about waiting in lines, and they are revealing of a person's overall attitude about their time and waste of their time:

1. **Waiting in lines is for other people but not for me.** I am smarter than most and can arrange my activities to reduce waiting, I can delegate it and have others do whatever requires standing in line for me, I can buy privilege and bypass lines. (At Disney, you can hire a private guide by the hour and be escorted to the front of every line. You can travel by private jet and never stand in a TSA security line. You can sign a power of attorney and send someone to the DMV line in your place. You can avoid going to restaurants that do not accept and honor reservations.)

2. **Waiting in lines is just a necessary part of life, and there's nothing to be done about it.** Patience is a virtue. Life is made up of random chance. Note: Acceptance of ordinary realities that are counter to deriving maximum benefit from your time equates to surrender of control.

3. **Somehow scheming to skip waiting in lines or paying to bypass lines is unfair** and unjust to everyone else and

Time People Spend Waiting in Line?, continued

something I *shouldn't* do. Having the idea that my time is more important than other people's is arrogant, egotistical, and shameful. Note: Guilt about creating benefit for yourself blocks any benefit coming to you.

Each of us chooses one of these three philosophical positions. Whichever you've chosen has been established in your subconscious mind as a governing, navigational principle lording authority over all your other decisions, largely without you being consciously aware of its influence.

CHAPTER 7

How to Turn Time into Wealth

There is only one success—to be able to spend your life in your own way.

—CHRISTOPHER MORLEY

T here is an old joke that says: "I've been rich and I've been poor. Rich is definitely better." Well, I concur. I make absolutely no apology for striving to be rich and for teaching and inspiring others to do the same. Furthermore, I believe you have every right to figure out ways to make maximum money from minimum time. When you can honestly apply the axiomatic advice of "work smarter, not harder," more power to you! I do not think any special heroism comes from earning your money through backbreaking work or long hours.

My Titanium Member Ron LeGrand, who has bought and "flipped" thousands of properties and teaches his real estate profit methods to thousands of investors each year, has a pet saying: "The less I do, the more I make." It is obviously open to misinterpretation. Ron works and does so cheerfully. But he has learned to focus on work that directly produces wealth.

I suspect I am unique in working up close, personal, hands-on with more than 500 first-generation millionaire and multi-millionaire entrepreneurs, most of whom built their wealth by creating and building new businesses from scratch, many of whom hit the million-dollar mark in a hurry. I have been in their offices, they in mine; had hundreds of hours of telephone conversations with them; worked with them individually and in groups; and had countless opportunities over years to observe their behavior and probe their psyches. My Renegade Millionaire System and once-a-year seminar I hold deal exclusively and extensively with what separates these "renegade millionaires" from the pack. (For more information about my system and seminars, go to www.renegademillionaire.com or accept the free gift offer on page 187.) One of the key factors in their success is the way they link time to money, and think in terms of investing time. Most, like Ron, are always looking for ways to get more for less, invest fewer minutes of work, extract more dollars.

One way they do this is by making themselves into bona fide experts in some field, one thing from which wealth can come. There is the old story about the customer angrily demanding an itemized bill from the plumber, who submitted a $250.00 bill for two minutes' work—smacking the clogged pipe with a hammer. The plumber wrote out the itemized bill as follows: For hitting pipe with hammer: $5.00. For knowing where to hit pipe with hammer: $245.00. Getting into that position—when you can be paid not (just) for what you do (physical labor) but for what you know (intellectual equity)—is a very worthy objective.

So, let there be no mistake. I think you deserve to be rich. I think you have a right to be rich. I think you provide enormous service to society by getting and being rich. I think government should be forbidden from penalizing or attacking you for being rich.

"On the Other Hand . . ."

With all that said, though, I have to suggest that money isn't everything.

It is a lot easier to give the "money isn't everything" and "money doesn't buy happiness" lecture after you have a considerable amount of money than before. Personally, I always resented hearing it when I was broke. And believe me, I understand that a person NEEDS a certain level of financial success before he can give a great deal of thought to the bigger philosophical issues of life. I think in our land of great opportunity, it is disgraceful not to do well. I don't see any honor in being poor. No shame in it as a temporary condition, but there should be shame if being poor is accepted as a permanent way of life. But, to be certain, money is only part, and maybe a small part, of "wealth."

On a surprisingly cool summer morning in Cleveland, Ohio, I sit in a dirty jog cart (the work-a-day version of a sulky), reins in hands, bouncing along behind an aging, mildly lame, Standardbred horse on the Northfield Park backstretch. Damp dirt, gravel, and bits of manure are kicked up past the mud screen onto my boots and pants, occasionally hitting my face. I am in seventh heaven. Of course, I'm just fooling around. But most of the folks there doing the same thing and taking care of these horses as work are in seventh heaven too. They couldn't imagine doing anything else. On this particular day and night, a 70-year-old man, Earl Bowman, and his wife, Joanna, were celebrating their 50th wedding anniversary. Earl, a retired driver and still a very good trainer, took his horse to the paddock, took care of it, and worked just as he would any other night. After the race, Joanna joined him as he led the horse into the winners' circle for the photo. Then he took the horse back to the barns where he had another hour's work ahead of him, stripping off the harness, bathing the horse, walking the horse to cool him out, bandaging the horse's legs, and so on. And if you asked Earl if he could have gone anywhere else or done anything else on that night, what would he wish for, he'd have no answer. *This* is wealth.

I am often asked what, of the varied but intertwined things I do, I like doing best. There is the speaking, to audiences as small as 250, as large as 25,000, for 60 minutes or 60 hours in a multiday seminar. At some of those engagements, I am sharing the day with celebrities, including ones I enjoy meeting, with top CEOs I find fascinating; at others, I'm solo. There is the private consulting, a day or two in a room isolated from the world, working with a client or client and his team. There is the development of advertising, marketing, and sales strategy and the copywriting for advertisements, webinars, radio commercials, TV infomercials, and direct-mail campaigns. There is the content writing for books like this, five monthly newsletters, weekly client group memos, home study courses. So, the oft-asked question: Of all the things I do, which do I like best?

My first answer is receiving and depositing the checks. Being very well compensated is what I enjoy best. I'm with Mark Twain on this: Nobody but a blockhead writes but for the money. And more is better. You will hear people say that they love what they do so much they would do it for free. I have yet to meet any wealthy person or top achiever who means it.

My second answer is more instructive: I do not dislike any of the things I do. On the few occasions that has occurred and I have found myself engaged in work or activity or relationships that I did not like, I changed the situation. Often abruptly. When I could afford doing so and when I couldn't. I have a high work ethic. I work a lot, and I convert a lot of work into a whale of a lot of money. This is only possible because I generally like the work I am doing and the conditions in which I'm doing it and the people I'm doing it for and with. It's very, very difficult to sustain performance and productivity for very long if any of those three things are reversed.

Wealth of this kind—liking your work, the conditions in which you work, and the people you work for and with—almost automatically begets financial wealth.

This does not mean it all has to be *fun*. As Larry Winget says, in the title of one of his blunt-force books, it's called work for a reason. And it's called a workplace for a reason. I am not a believer in the playground, happy place, come 'n go as you please approach that you find at Google. The Happiest Place on Earth, Disney, does not run its workplace that way, and I'm siding with Disney. The insistence that your work has to be just as much fun as an evening at the circus is ridiculous. And, if you are going to be successful, you are going to be engaged in a myriad of unfun and even uninteresting things that are necessary to facilitate the important, interesting, productive, and profitable things. There's nothing fun or interesting to me about travel, but if I am to stand in front of an audience that can't be brought to me, and collect a lot of money for it, and I make that choice, I am going to have to suffer an airplane flight, a limo driver who wants to tell me his life story, and a hotel bed that makes my back ache. You avoid, change, replace, automate, and delegate what you can, but so far, for me to be there, I have to go there. Yes, I know I can Skype, and we do broadcast live and prerecorded webinars, but to date, nobody's willing to pay me $50,000.00 to $100,000.00 to Skype it in. Every business has the same kind of elements that the operator considers no fun but still must do. Everything one likes doing has a price tag attached.

The idea of succeeding by pursuing your number-one passion is also a pile of B.S. Success for entrepreneurs is, first and foremost, market driven, and there are marketplace realities that must be dealt with. Not all passions offer productivity or profit. There is usually some way to integrate what passionately interests you with a business, but it can't necessarily be the business or the way a business decision is made. An entrepreneur's time and other resources must be invested where there is excellent profit, if not the best possible profit. That is the prime consideration.

Ultimately, it's pointless to invest your time in pursuing success doing something you fundamentally dislike. Success is not just about how much money you can make, but, also, maybe more so, how you make the money. That is what this book is really about. There is no shortage of opportunities, or of clients, customers, or patients. Some, maybe many, may prove unwilling to cooperate with the way you want to make money. But others will. I am often told about this book's recommendations and my other rules of engagement, about the way I make my money, that they are impractical for others. They disqualify themselves for all sorts of silly reasons, not the least of which is the delusion that I am special. For the record, I'm a high school graduate who never attended college, with zero formal training or apprenticeship in anything. Everything I've grown to do so well that I have long lines of people willing to pay princely sums for and willing to do business with me on my terms, I was bad at when I started. The processes of going from dumb to smart, inept to exceptionally capable, barely knowledgeable to expert, unknown to respected and/or to celebrity, as well as the processes for autonomy are all well-known, well-documented, and repeated constantly by large numbers of people. You can invest your time in those processes or invest the same time in making the list of all the ways your business is different, your opportunities are fewer, your handicaps greater.

You can also invest time just in getting rich, but at the expense of your autonomy. Or you can invest time in getting wealthy.

Many people manage to get rich, but comparatively few get wealthy. As long as you're going to put in your time on the planet, why not invest it in a way that makes you *wealthy?*

Napoleon Hill, most famous for his classic best-selling book, *Think and Grow Rich,* spent his entire life encouraging people to pursue great goals, including financial riches. Hill was originally sent out on his mission by America's first billionaire, Andrew Carnegie, who believed there were "universal principles of success" that could be taught and learned, just as any other collection of mechanical skills could be learned. Carnegie helped get Hill in-depth interviews and relationships with hundreds of the greatest achievers of that era. Hill identified 13 commonalities, and wrote about them, first in *The Laws of Success,* then in *Think and Grow Rich.* Following publication of that book in 1937, Napoleon Hill lectured, trained large sales organizations, recorded inspirational messages, and, in various ways, distributed his "science of success" based on those 13 principles.

Late in his life, Napoleon Hill wrote another book I highly recommend: *Grow Rich with Peace of Mind.* In this book, after acquiring great riches, losing great riches, and a long career, Napoleon Hill did his best to reconcile the issues of pursuing great financial success and achieving total wealth, in the bigger, broader sense.

How Much Is Enough?

So, how do you turn time into wealth? Reverse engineering. Decide what "wealth" means to you. This includes what I call your "enough is enough number"—the total of investable assets you need to feel secure and spin off sufficient income to support you and your family as you wish to live. Not at wild-fantasy, win-the-lottery, own-a-castle-in-Spain levels, at least not for most people, but a reasonable yet desirable level. Develop a clear, detailed picture of what your life would look like and how you would live if you had that "number" in place. Does this picture include a second home or a big vacation twice a year or owning a bed-and-breakfast? In this picture, how do you use, spend, and invest your time?

Once you have this entire picture built, with detailed clarity, you can begin looking backward, to where you are now. You identify the obstacles in the path and begin looking for and thinking about all the possible ways they might be removed. You can construct a plan. Establish yearly, monthly, and weekly targets and benchmarks. Then, most important of all, you can judge whether your present moment's choices made with your time are linked to creating the wealth you desire.

CHAPTER 8

How to Handle the
Information Avalanche

I had a great idea this morning, but I didn't like it.

—SAM GOLDWYN

S upposedly, we are in the Paperless Age. But, according to University Microfilms, we're now creating *one billion pages* of information each and every day here in the United States alone. Sometimes I think most of it crosses *my* desk!

People are struggling to cope with the avalanche of information. I get as big an avalanche as anybody. Here's what goes on, for me. First of all, I have all the trade and professional journals, new books, association newsletters, and other documents related to my three primary businesses—direct marketing, freelance copywriting, and speaking—to keep up with. I have all the general business press to be concerned with, from *Entrepreneur* and *Inc.* to *Forbes, Fortune,* and *The Wall*

Street Journal. As a consultant, I'm often "learning" several new businesses in connection with my clients, so I read their trade publications too. Because of the infomercial business, I watch a lot of TV, and I review about 20 hours of videotape every month. Because I do so much work with direct mail, I read ALL of my "junk mail." And I read at least one book a week. Fortunately, I speed read. But, still . . .

That doesn't even include the avalanche moving to you online. I avoid it myself, but I know you won't. There's nothing different about it, except its immediacy and more aggressive intrusiveness. It's up to you to route *all* your incoming and in-bound through a screening process and method of organization. Just because it's accessible online doesn't mean you should access it online. It may be that somebody should be fetching, printing it out, or condensing it for you. Just because it wants to flow to you online and even demand response from you online doesn't mean you have to permit it to have its way with you.

How Do You Handle All This?

I'm sure you are digging out from under your own avalanche of information every day, too. Let me offer you some "shovels."

Improve Your Reading Skills

Many people are poor readers and insist that they do not "like" to read. Sadly, our U.S. universities and high schools alike are churning out massive numbers of young people who do not read, get all their news from TV or radio, or quick, abbreviated online reports, and, in a shocking number of cases, are borderline illiterate. Once again, honesty with yourself is the best policy. Hire a tutor if necessary. If not, then take or get a good home-study speed reading course. Although I'm self-taught, when people ask me to recommend courses, I refer them to Howard Berg. You may have seen Howard on TV. He holds the Guinness Book of World Records title of World's Fastest Reader. You can get information about Howard's courses on speed reading, accelerated learning, and memory at www.howardbergspeedreading.com. Speed reading (and speed comprehension) is real.

By the way, I think you MUST read, as you can see in the accompanying article (Figure 8.1 on page 106) that I originally wrote for one of my newsletters.

At Least Be Sure You Get the Information You Really Want and Need

If you are really busy and time is much more of an issue than money, you can pay others to read for you. There are "clipping services," including one run by *The Wall Street Journal*, that will ferret through hundreds of daily newspapers, trade magazines, and other media for the topic you have requested and fax to you just the articles about your topic. You may have a staff person read and clip for you. A good project for son, daughter, grandson, granddaughter is a regular pile of reading, like trade journals, to clip, highlight, even summarize for you. One of my clients pays his high-school-age son $75.00 a week to read 14 different trade journals and newsletters and record summaries and excerpts on a weekly CD that he can listen to while he drives to work.

Set Aside Any "Bulk" Material that Is Not Time Sensitive, to Review at Your Leisure

Catalogs, interesting-looking junk mail, and popular magazines fall into this category. You MUST be very selective about what warrants your attention now, what later, what never.

Consider Condensation

You can subscribe to *Executive Book Summaries*, for example, and get brief summaries of a dozen new, "hot" business books every

FIGURE 8.1

APPARENTLY, YOU ARE NOW AN AMAZING ODDITY AKIN TO A THREE-HEADED COW – IF YOU READ. The Saturday after Christmas, working in my office, I had the weekend *Today Show* on the TV, and jerked my head around to watch when I heard this amazing statement, delivered with breathless excitement:

> "Coming up next – we'll interview the woman who read a
> book a week for a year and has written her own book
> about the experience!

What!?! With brief lapses here and there, I've read at least a book a week every year for more than 30 years. What's the big deal about this? Well, apparently it is a big deal. The last time I went to Barnes & Noble, I bought a new biography of Ben Franklin, Tom Peters' new book, a couple of other business books, a book about stroke-free living, three paperback novels to take when traveling, and about 20 magazines. The clerk said: "Lifetime's supply, huh?" Sheesh.

You MUST read a lot to succeed. Here are the reasons: (1) Varied, diverse input, ideas, viewpoints, life stories, examples, all the essential raw material poured into your subconscious mind, for it to sift, sort, try matching up with other puzzle pieces it already has, so it can occasionally yell "Eureka!" and hand you something profitable – without daily flow of new stuff, it just sleeps. Wealth secret: you cannot manufacture anything without raw material. Not even money. (2) Without exposure to others' thinking, your own range of thought shrinks. Soon, you're a mental midget. Your range of thought narrows, like range of motion shrinks if you don't move and stretch. (3) You can't stay current. I read a monstrous amount and I still can't stay current. If you're not reading a book or two, a dozen magazines, a few newspapers, and a few newsletters every week, you must be way, way, way behind. Pretty soon, your conversation reveals you as a dinosaur. (4) If you have kids, you want to set a decent example for them. They need to see you reading. They need to hear you talking about what you read. When I was a kid, the years my family was dead broke, we made a regular scheduled, weekly trek to the public library for an hour or so. My father, mother, and I each picked out three or four books for the week, took them home, read them, and talked about them. Now I prefer going to the bookstore, because I have money, and like keeping the books. However, I'm grateful for the library-habit years. It would be a better thing for most families to do than going to the movies, arcade, or Wal-Mart.

Historical note I had in a book I wrote back in 1985: the town leaders of Franklin, Massachusetts, once wrote and asked Ben Franklin for a donation so they could buy a bell for the church steeple. He sent money with this note: "I'm honored you have named your town Franklin and a donation is enclosed. However, I suggest you start a library with it rather than buying a bell. I prefer sense to sound."

month. This is sort of a *Cliff Notes* for adults. There's a similar service, *Newstrack,* for news buffs.

Online, there are services like Google Alerts, to notify you of information relevant to you. You can go to most news sites, trade journal sites, and information sites and access by topic search.

One small caution: Don't completely close off spontaneous discovery and eclectic interests. You may want to raid *The New York Times* website daily just for any news specifically relevant to your business, but it is still good now and then to read the *Sunday New York Times* cover to cover. You find useful things you never knew existed.

Use Your DVR, TiVo, On-Demand Services, Etc.

No one is really bound anymore by the TV schedule. You need not be home at 9:00 P.M. to watch the documentary on CNBC about a company of interest to you airing at 9:00 P.M. In defense of TV, often slammed as the crap box, there happens to be a lot of useful, instructive, and provocative programming for entrepreneurs. Of the general crop airing as I write this, I like and recommend the ABC show *Shark Tank.* But the financial cable channels are full of worthwhile programming. There may also be a reality show in your business niche.

Use Your "Drive Time" or Travel Time as Learning Time

Here are the average to-and-from-the-office commute times for major cities: New York, 1 hour, 5 minutes; Washington, DC, 1 hour; Houston, 1 hour; Los Angeles, 1 hour, 30 minutes; Dallas, 48 minutes; Phoenix, 46 minutes; Buffalo, 40 minutes. That can be classroom time. All my best teaching is available on audio CD (www.DanKennedy.com/store), and most sales, marketing, and business experts offer their training on CD as well. Many new business books are also released on CD. Your 40 minutes in the car per day x 250 business days a year + well-selected audio programs = 167 classroom hours available to you.

Resist the Siren Song of Distraction

A lot of people let "noninformation" consume a lot of their time. Today's news is tomorrow's fish-wrap, yet we have just about become consumed with useless news. Twenty-four-hour-a-day news stations. News-talk radio. News and opinion websites. Yes, you want to be informed. But do you need to be informed about the latest celebrity sex or shoplifting scandal, the latest athlete going to jail, the weather in Bulgaria?

Specialize. But Not Too Much

It is probably better to know a great deal about one, two, or several things than a tiny bit about everything. Specialization almost always adds value. And it can be used to limit information flow.

In business, I specialize in direct-response advertising and direct mail, with a subspecialty in "long form" (copy-intensive) advertising, and another subspecialty in the marketing of information products. As a result, I rarely bother reading *Advertising Age* magazine, a trade journal for traditional advertising professionals, but I do read *Direct Marketing* magazine and *TARGET*. Being able NOT to read something is very useful.

However, too narrow a focus becomes myopia. If you exclude too much information and input, you rob your brain of the raw material needed for breakthrough ideas. Most people in a particular industry are so myopic they start committing what I call "marketing incest"—with the same result as real incest; after just a few generations, everybody's stupid. People in "x" business look at what everybody else in "x" business is doing. They go to association meetings together, read the same trade journals, and copy from each other. Getting outside this box is important.

So, you need a balance. A lot of specialization, but not too much specialization.

Dealing with today's overwhelming quantity of information is a bit like looking for the proverbial needle in a haystack. That task is made less daunting because you know you are looking for a needle. It would be even worse if you were just told to go through the entire hay mound and look for *something*.

So, here's a little test (Figure 8.2 on page 110) I give to my clients that you might try taking at the end of each week. It will help you focus, help you spot the right things, and help you find the needles in the haystack of the week ahead.

If you actually discipline yourself to get one answer to each question worth putting down in writing just once a week, after a year, you'll be 624 big steps ahead of your peers and competitors. And the odds are excellent you'll have uncovered a few ultra-valuable gems. Keeping these questions in the forefront of your mind is a way of "electrifying and magnetizing your antenna" so casual conversations or even an overheard conversation can yield something useful you'd otherwise never have noticed.

How to Organize and Manage Ideas

The great success educator Earl Nightingale wrote:

> "A single thought can revolutionize your life. A single thought can make you rich or well-to-do, or it can land you in prison for the rest of your life. Everything was an idea before it became real in the world . . . the law of averages begins to swing in your direction when you begin to produce ideas."

"Ideas," Earl said, "are like slippery fish."

> It is up to us to catch every idea—not to let one slip by us.

For many years, I used a strategy adapted from Michael Vance, a close associate of Walt

FIGURE 8.2

What Do You Know This Week, That You Didn't Know Last Week, About...

1. Your business? _____

_____

2. Your industry as a whole? _____

_____

3. Your competitors? _____

_____

4. Your customers or clients as a group? _____

_____

5. Your top 10, 20, or 30 customers or clients? _____

_____

6. A client, individually? _____

_____

7. One of the top leaders in your field? _____

_____

8. Societal, cultural, or economic trends that may affect your business? _____

_____

9. A "success" topic – personal finance, self-motivation, time management? _____

_____

10. A "marketing" topic – direct- response advertising, construction of offers, copy that sells, direct-mail, the Internet?

_____

11. A person, event, or topic in the current news of great interest or importance to your clientele? _____

_____

12. A "method" – a means, process, technique of doing something useful to you, whether manufacturing your widget faster or making a sales presentation more effectively? _____

_____

Disney, called "the storyboard." I had a corked wall in my office, with vertical columns, each column headed by a business or project title. Then, every time I had an idea, I'd jot it down on a small card, about half of a 3-by-5-inch card, and pushpin it up there in the correct column. I carried a little supply of cards with me at all times, so I never lost an idea. Frankly, for a while, I drifted away from that; now I've returned.

I also maintain different "project notebooks" or even legal pads dedicated to one project.

I have a pad and pen everywhere. Even in the bathroom.

Some people are very adept at verbalizing their ideas, so they carry micro-recorders, dictate, have a staff person or service transcribe it all, then organize it. My brain engages with pen in hand or fingers on keyboard.

The important thing is for you to choose and use some method for capturing every idea that comes to you, wherever and whenever it happens.

Bulk is a problem for many of us. My friend Lee Milteer has research, reference, and project piles in gigantic clear plastic bags, so she can see what's in them. My piles have 4-by-6-inch title cards on then. I have more than 1,000 books on shelves, but if I read a book with only a few worthwhile pages, I tear out the pages, file them, then throw out the book. The computer obviously provides a means of reducing bulk for information storage. For many people, the dictionary and thesaurus have been replaced by the online dictionary. A bookcase full of encyclopedia with Wikipedia. You can certainly do that with your own ideas and content as well. I'm now able to discard a small mountain of notes after finishing writing a book, keeping only what transferred into a computer file.

From a time standpoint, the trick is to be able to find what you need when you need it.

How the Well-Trained, Conditioned, and Fit Subconscious Mind Helps Handle the Information Avalanche

From the mid-1950s to 1960, Dr. Maxwell Maltz worked devising and perfecting practical methods for making the subconscious mind fitter and more useful. His work is summarized in his classic best-selling book *Psycho-Cybernetics* and in the updated companion I co-authored, *The New Psycho-Cybernetics.* Dr. Maltz's findings and methods have been of enormous importance to me my entire life, and I urge you to investigate them for yourself. Specific to being more productive, and to better managing and utilizing information, you can deliberately make your subconscious work better as a finder, organizer, and provider of whatever you need to make a presentation, write a sales letter, whatever. This is beyond ordinary memory. This is a creative retrieval process.

Dan Kennedy's #7 No B.S. Time Truth

If you don't MANAGE information, you can't profit from information.

For example, I, like most direct-response ad copywriters, maintain a room full of what we call "swipe files." These are files of samples by category. One file contains "Headlines, Weight Loss Ads," another "Headlines, Income Opportunity Ads." There are files for opening sentences, guarantees, offers, and on and on. Hundreds and hundreds and hundreds of them. Huge notebooks. Reference books. It takes a lot of time to go through all the relevant ones physically in preparing to write copy for a client. Sometimes that's unavoidable, but quite often, for me, it is not. Instead, I give my subconscious mind the assignment of going through its stored "swipe files" to find the right idea, "hook," or starting point for a particular ad—*while I sleep!* When I wake, the idea spews out through my fingers onto my computer screen. This is not a happy accident or some freakish mind mutation unique to me. It is the result of deliberate training with Psycho-Cybernetics. It probably liberates me from at least 20 hours of hard labor every month.

CHAPTER 9

Fire Yourself, Replace Yourself, Make More Money, and Have More Fun

You all look like happy campers to me. Happy campers you are, happy campers you have been and, as far as I'm concerned, happy campers you will always be.

—Vice-President Dan Quayle, Addressing a Group of Samoans

There are all sorts of things that make entrepreneurs unhappy. We detest government interference, government red tape, and government stupidity. Vendors who fail to keep commitments or meet quality standards make us unhappy. Bankers and lawyers bring us much unhappiness. (Risky these days to joke about terrorists, but maybe you heard of the terrorists who hijacked a plane full of lawyers returning from a convention. The terrorists warned that, if their demands were not met, they'd release ten lawyers every hour.) But, above all else, the thing that makes entrepreneurs most miserable— although they may not easily recognize it—is *routine*.

Entrepreneurs make lousy managers and administrators because too much of that work is routine.

This tells you a lot about what you must do in order to achieve maximum success, derive maximum value from your time, and lead the happiest possible life: You must systematically, aggressively divest yourself of those activities you do not do well, do not do happily, or find routine so as to systematically invest your time (and talent, knowledge, know-how, and other resources) in those things you do extraordinarily well, enjoy doing, and find intellectually stimulating.

I have just described for you a formula for peak personal productivity, as a specialist. And you ought to note that, in every field of enterprise, specialists outearn generalists ten to one. Heart surgeons vs. M.D.s. Sophisticated database computer program developers vs. programmers. Nuclear waste disposal experts vs. garbage men. And so on.

But having said that, how do we make that happen? How do we get there? It certainly is easier said than done. But you can start moving in this direction today, step by step, just as I have.

"We're Overpaying Him, But He's Worth It"

The movie magnate Samuel Goldwyn, famous for butchering the language, said that. Actually, your business is overpaying you for some of the jobs you do and grossly underpaying you for others.

Step One: Honest Self-Analysis and Self-Understanding

The typical entrepreneur—yourself included—believes, no, knows, absolutely *knows* that he can do anything and everything, because, at some point in time, we have had to. However, even though I can do it all, truth is, there are only a few things I do so extraordinarily well that—even if given all the money in the world—I wouldn't hire anybody else to do them. There are only a few things I do better than anybody else on the planet. Truth be told, you have only a few things in that category too. Then, you and I have another couple of handfuls of things we do well, better than most, but cannot be considered our "specialties." And there are any number of things you and I do that we do out of necessity, don't do very well, but do them anyway.

If you're honest with yourself, you can create these three lists. (And it's a very productive exercise to sit down alone and make these three lists.)

"Delegate or Stagnate"

Step Two: Delegation

Of course, delegating is as hard for entrepreneurs as telling the truth is for politicians. It's downright unnatural. Why? Habit, for one thing. We create our businesses from scratch, do it all, develop a way of doing things that we believe in, and find that habit is hard to break. No one is ever going to do things exactly the same way we do them.

Jay Van Andel, cofounder of the giant Amway Corporation, impressed me many years ago with a speech titled "Delegate or Stagnate." Of course, the entire Amway system is based on multiplication of effort; one person learning a set of skills, then duplicating himself over and over again. And Jay and his partner, Rich DeVos, had a business that grew like topsy. In order to stay ahead of it, they constantly delegated and—ultimately—replaced themselves over and over again, which we'll get to in a minute. What Jay made very clear to me is that the only way to advance in any business is to keep delegating.

THERE'S MORE THAN ONE WAY TO BE RIGHT

Brendan Suhr, the assistant head coach of the Detroit Pistons during their championship years in the 1980s, said to me:

Do you know how many head coaches there are in the NBA? Well, there are at least that many different ways to be right, because every one of these coaches does things differently, yet they all represent the top 1/10% of the coaching profession. There are 1,000 guys who'd like every one of these jobs. There are at least 100 guys who'd be good candidates for every one of these jobs. So these head coaches all do it "right," yet they all do it differently.

His point is valid.

You cannot delegate if you believe there's only one way to get things done right.

OFTEN, GOOD ENOUGH IS GOOD ENOUGH

Let me give you an example: I used to have a business associate, a key person in my company, a $100,000.00-a-year guy— whose time had to be worth more than $250.00 an hour. It so happened he had a fetish about how boxes were packed. When we were leaving for a weeklong series of seminars, instead of attending to any number of important responsibilities, he'd be back in the shipping department for hours, doing the job of the $10.00-an-hour shipping clerk. I've got to admit that he packed a wicked box. I mean, this guy's boxes were works of art. They were very, very carefully packed, firm to the top and the corners, so that no corner crumpled in. The tape was perfectly straight.

Dan Kennedy's #8 No B.S. Time Truth

Good enough is good enough.

The bottom and sides were taped just as perfectly as the top. Every label was on straight. However, in the many years since he has been gone, our shipping clerks shipped thousands of cartons to my seminar sites. Not packed quite as well. Corners crumpled a little bit now and again. Tape crooked. Labels cockeyed. But every one of these boxes got there. The product was fine. The result was the same. Good enough is good enough.

Many, many things can be delegated to people who will not do them the way you would, won't do them as perfectly as you would, but will wind up with the same result. Every one of these things should be delegated. In fact, you MUST delegate. You cannot move ahead without jettisoning some responsibilities and tasks in order to make room for new, more valuable tasks and responsibilities.

And I'm not necessarily talking about creating a giant managerial bureaucracy. Today, you can delegate to independent contractors, freelancers, and vendors too. Outsourcing is the buzzword of the day, with good reason. Also, if you have anybody around you with intelligence and talent, you must keep giving them new, more important responsibilities and getting them to delegate.

MASTERING DELEGATION

You MUST master this difficult skill. To delegate effectively, here's the seven-step process.

1. Define what is to be done.
2. Be certain the delegatee understands what is to be done.
3. Explain why it is to be done as you are prescribing it to be done.
4. Teach how it is to be done without micro-micro-managing.
5. Be sure the delegatee understands the how-to process.
6. Set the deadline for completion or progress report.

7. Be sure you have agreement to the date or time and method.

By the way, resisting the temptation to micro-manage will require plenty of willpower. One of a number of reasons I stayed out of my business offices and worked at home as much as possible was because when I went to the office, I was "drawn" to listen in on, interfere with, or critique every phone call, look at every fax, poke my nose all the way into everything—to the extent that I ruined everybody else's productivity as well as my own. Today, I am never there. In fact, I am most often in a home office at the opposite end of the country from the office where my sole staff person does everything.

This is not rocket science. But it takes very deliberate patience. It even takes time. But investing time in getting good at this and getting people around you who respond to it is the only way to get time freed up to do more valuable things yourself.

Going Beyond Delegation

And, as difficult as all this is, it's just the beginning. The real, big, blockbuster secret of entrepreneurial success and happiness goes beyond delegation to replacement.

Step Three: Replacing Yourself

Rory Fatt, president of Restaurant Marketing Systems, exhorts the thousands of restaurant owners he advises: "Fire yourself! You'll make more money and have more fun." The disease exists in every industry, but Rory says it's epidemic and endemic in restaurants—owners terminally inflicted with the belief that they must be the one making the sauce, greeting the guests at the door, doing the inventory. They are so busy doing the $10.00-an-hour jobs, they never get to do the $100.00-an-hour job: marketing to bring in new customers and to keep customers coming back. Rory says you can hire just about anybody to wash glasses, and there are a lot of people you can hire to make the sauce, but there's hardly anybody you can hire to effectively market and promote the restaurant.

"They Gave Me a Lifetime Contract, Then They Pronounced Me Legally Dead"

I agree with Rory—most business owners need to fire themselves from a lot of those $10.00-an-hour jobs. The late college basketball coach Jim Valvano wrote a book long before his death from cancer with the above title as a sardonic poke at his field. It's said there are only three kinds of coaches: those just getting hired, those just fired, and those soon to be fired. Jimmy Johnson took the Dallas Cowboys to two Super Bowls in a row, then was fired. Nobody, and I mean nobody, is indispensable. The day Johnny Carson retired, the entire country wondered if the *Tonight Show* would soon die. So did NBC. But we have become loyal to Jay Leno, and a whole lot of people might not recognize Johnny Carson if they bumped into him on the street. Jack Paar couldn't even get onto the studio property without an ID card. As I am writing this, Leno, with the largest audience in late night, atop NBC's most successful franchise, is being forced out for the second time. They did it once before, had the Conan debacle, and brought Leno back. No one is ever safe. Since it's your business, you probably are. You don't have to fire you. But there are times you should.

Step Four: Welcoming Your Dispensability

Most people do not like the idea of dispensability. The entrepreneur on vacation is schizophrenic: hoping everything is OK at the office but disappointed when he calls in and finds out everything is OK. How can things be running smoothly without him? I'm going to try and sell you on welcoming your own dispensability.

Entrepreneurs grow in experience and expertise very quickly. Fast learners. You will probably master entire "chunks" of a business in a matter of months, yet you may continue doing those same functions for years. This will lead to stagnation and unhappiness. You may even wind up ineffectively doing things you could do well just out of boredom. The ultimate answer is replacement. That is, you replace yourself and step up to a new set of opportunities and responsibilities. You groom someone to take your place.

Note that this is the opposite of executive behavior in a corporate bureaucracy. In that environment, the executive is desperately afraid of the up-and-comers who would take over his job. The executive is determined to protect his turf. Through secrecy, deliberate confusion, corporate politics, and every other imaginable method, the executive tries to make himself indispensable. The super-savvy entrepreneur does the opposite and tries to make himself dispensable.

I have gone through many different scenarios in my business life. I had 42 employees; then for quite a while five; now only one. I have delegated a lot, I've delegated almost nothing, and done everything myself. I confess I am still guilty of doing some menial tasks myself rather than supervise anyone. Beginning in 1999, I aggressively switched from delegation to replacement of a sort. I sold my information products business then. In 2003, I sold my newsletter business. I've arrived at what I call my "Dan as Center of Universe Strategy": me in the middle and satellite businesses owned and managed by others all based on me, my writings, my other content, all paying me. Right now, there are four such satellites.

A good question to consider is, what plan are you working on to reduce your business's and income's dependency on your own time and effort?

What to Do with the Time You Liberate

One thing you can do is enjoy the success you create. Golf, buy racehorses and hang out at the track (a passion of mine), write, get involved in community service or politics, whatever.

Dan Kennedy's #9 No B.S. Time Truth

Liberation is the ultimate entrepreneurial achievement.

If you're looking for the answer that turns your time into the most money and wealth possible, then turn your attention to marketing. Get free of as many other aspects of your business as you can, get passionately interested in and good at marketing, and invest your time there. Why? Because it is infinitely easier to find or train someone to take care of a business's operations than it is to get someone to do its marketing. Marketing is the highest-paid profession and most valuable part of a business. The person who can create systems for acquiring customers, clients, or patients effectively and profitably is the "money person." He is the equivalent of a "high impact" or "franchise" player in sports.

Let me give you a quick example: A big publisher of a variety of different newsletters, on average, hires and pays only four or five professional copywriters each year to write the sales letters that acquire new subscribers for those newsletters. The copywriter who can create a successful sales letter for this company will rarely be paid less than $250,000.00 in a year, in fees and royalties—for writing just one letter! Find me any other kind of writer who can command $250,000.00 for eight pages. You can't find a novelist. A screenwriter. A technical writer. A journalist. No one gets $250,000.00 for eight pages.

In my book *Make Millions with Your Ideas* (Plume/Dutton), I tell the story of the turnaround of the now-famous Thighmaster from a terribly unsuccessful product to a huge, megamillions of dollars success. The person who figured out the three "little" things to do to "fix" that product's marketing (described in my book) received millions of dollars.

Now I have what should be very exciting news: mMost of the top-flight, most successful marketing wizards are entrepreneurs who grew up into marketers and who are self-taught, many in very short periods of time. What they have done to become what they are—people whose time is worth thousands of dollars per hour—you can do too. Yes, I am here to tell you that you can, over a two-to-five-year term, make your hours each worth thousands or even tens of thousands of dollars.

Join me. Free yourself from boring routine and modest pay-off activity and graduate to life as a "Master Marketer."

Refuse to Fetch

The uninformed are always asking me to fetch something. I get requests from people I barely know to read their book manuscripts and offer a favorable comment they can use—then they ask me to go and fetch the book in a pdf online. People ask me to go to their websites and watch a video and critique it for them. Even people eager to sell me something tell me to fetch their information.

My dog likes playing fetch. I am not a dog.

I often wind up choosing who I'll do business with because one puts needed information in my hands while others competing for my patronage ask me to fetch. I never respond to a request for a favor requiring me to play fetch before I can grant it. It's up to you to put everything I need in front of me, including your fax number and address, so I can respond the way I want to respond, without the need to look up or hunt for your contact information. I am not chasing *any* balls.

You may prefer email, and that's your prerogative. Whoever has the upper hand gets to dictate. But know that when others ask you to play fetch, they steal your time. If you surrender, you surrender time from a finite and dwindling supply. People who want things from you—cooperation, favors, money—can reasonably be required not to ask you to fetch for them.

Many people are utterly unaware of how much of their time is given over to fetching. They just fall into doing it without thinking, because it seems commonplace, because "that's the way it's

Refuse to Fetch, continued

done," because others will think them odd or old-fashioned or "difficult," because they fail to properly value their time.

The week I was writing this, my mail included a letter from a charity I have supported asking for donations for a particular purpose tied to an upcoming event, and offering going to a website, viewing a video, and there completing or downloading a response form. It was a lot faster to toss the appeal in the trash.

As an aside, two groups of consumers are most resistant to fetching: leading-edge boomers and seniors, and the exceptionally affluent. If you want their patronage, you have to be especially careful about asking them to go fetch. I recommend my books *No B.S. Guide to Marketing to Leading-Edge Boomers & Seniors* and *No B.S. Guide to Trust-Based Marketing.*

CHAPTER 10

The Link between Productivity
and Association

*Be courteous to all, but intimate with few, and let those few be
well tried before you give them your confidence.*

—GEORGE WASHINGTON, 1783

You can't actually manage time. The phrase "time
management" is inaccurate shorthand. You can only
manage things that affect your ability to convert time to
value, like environment, access, and all the other things discussed
in this book. One of the most significant, that you can control to
a great extent, is association—your choices of who you permit
into your world, who you give time to or invest time with, who
you look to for ideas, information, and education. The people
around you rarely have neutral effect. They either facilitate your
accomplishment, they undermine it, or they outright sabotage it.

The first useful association tactic is the elimination of toxic
people and saboteurs. It is not an easy thing to face facts about
a friend, family member, long-time employee, or long-time

vendor when they are, in some way, interfering with or just disapproving of your accomplishment. It is important to face these facts and to act on them because the more time you spend with people who are unhelpful, unsupportive, disrespectful, envious, resentful, bring a bleak and discouraging world view, or dysfunctional or outright damaging to you, the less value *all* your time has. These people don't just harm the minutes you and they are in the same place. Association is such a powerful thing we can't just switch it on and off like a light switch. Few people can so perfectly compartmentalize that they can lock every thought, assertion, and act of a toxic person in a little mind box and without leakage into other mind boxes. Paraphrasing a Chinese proverb (I found in a fortune cookie), if you lie down with mongrel dogs, even for a short nap, you wake up with fleas—and they ride with you wherever you go. Ideas, beliefs, opinions, and habits work just like that. Even if you are associating with someone who is intellectually or emotionally toxic, or with someone who is feckless and inept, only occasionally and briefly, it's enough time for the fleas to leap from them to you, burrow in, and be carried away by you, to subtly affect your performance and productivity. If your creativity or constructive thinking or work performance is thus diminished, so is the value of your time.

People who are detrimental for you to associate with are not necessarily evil or of evil intent. They may all be "good people," but that doesn't mean they're good for you. Good chocolate cake is not good for a diabetic. In fact, it's poison. As a diabetic myself, I can tell you that getting yourself to understand and accept that such food is poison and consistently acting on that knowledge require super-human effort. Getting those around you to accept it is even harder. But associating with somebody who is always pushing it to you, saying "Well, just have a tiny piece" is just as suicidal as baking it for yourself.

There are lots of ways a person can be toxic and poisonous to you. In my first marriage, my wife had a habit of picking a fight that could not be finished immediately before my departure for an important meeting or presentation. I've had clients describe how recurring disputes with a particular employee were mentally exhausting but couldn't be helped because, otherwise, that person was a great asset. The "otherwise" is a big problem. Many small businesses wind up with a ruthlessly defensive key person who goes into murder mode anytime an attempt is made to add a second person, but is "otherwise" terrific. There is the "we tried that before" guy. If it were up to him, we'd light the place with candles 'cuz Edison would have been limited to one try. There's the "constructive critic," always making you feel inadequate or undeserving, in the guise of being a cautionary ally worrying over you stubbing a toe. There are the Time Vampires described in an earlier chapter.

On the other hand, constructive association with creative, inspiring, encouraging, can-do people can do a great deal to bolster your performance, thus making your time more valuable.

Each minute of your time is made more or less valuable by the condition of your mind, and it is constantly being conditioned by association.

The entrepreneur is particularly susceptible to gaining or losing power by association because he has so many diverse responsibilities and is often operating under pressure, duress, and urgency. Playing this game in a compromised mental state, weakened or wounded by poor ideas and attitudes seeded into the mind by association, is extremely difficult. Playing it strengthened and empowered by rich ideas and attitudes seeded into the mind by association can make the difficult easy.

Simply put, you want to deliberately reduce and restrict the amount of your time left vulnerable to random thought or association, and deliberately, sharply reduce the amount of time given to association with people who won't make any productive contribution and may do harm. Does that mean you can only spend time with people you are in complete philosophical agreement with? No. In fact, such isolationism can be dangerous. But it does mean you should avoid association with people who believe and promulgate beliefs diametrically opposed to "success orientation." If you feel obligated to attend the family picnic and encounter folks of this ilk, nothing says you can't arrive late and leave early. Truth be told, your being included is probably done as much by obligation as is your attending. I'm sorry to say that the success-oriented individual is an irritant to many other people he may be related to by blood; linked to by long-time, largely accidental friendship; by church, civic activity, neighborhood; or some similar connection. The success-oriented entrepreneur, alone in a group of nonachievement-oriented civilians, is disturbing to them in much the same way a skinny person who can eat anything and not gain weight or even a fit person who exerts considerable discipline and effort to stay that way is to a group of overweight people.

You want to deliberately increase the amount of your time directed at chosen thinking and input, and constructive, productive association. You want to associate with strivers and achievers, with winners and champions. This is an uplifting force that translates into peak performance, which makes all your time more valuable.

Tapping into a "Mastermind"

One of the most effective formats for constructive association is the mastermind group. Participating in one or even several such groups—carefully chosen—is a specific recommendation that I have for you. This is an organized process for greatly heightened productivity and greatly accelerated speed of accomplishment that has its roots at the turn of the century. You need a bit of its background to fully appreciate its importance.

The Mastermind Concept is widely credited to the author Napoleon Hill, who developed it based on personal conversations with and investigations into leaders of America's great industrial age, such as Andrew Carnegie, Henry Ford, Harvey Firestone, and Thomas Edison. Hill is best known for his book *Think and Grow Rich* researched from 1917 to its publication in 1937. It is still a strong seller today, almost entirely by word-of-mouth. It, Ayn Rand's *Atlas Shrugged,* and the Bible are the three books most frequently referenced as life-altering works by top CEOs and entrepreneurs in surveys year after year.

I have a long history with Hill and his work, including involvement with the TV infomercial in the late 1980s that brought new attention to *Think and Grow Rich* and rather coincidentally launched Tony Robbins on TV. In 2013, I received The Persistence Award from the Napoleon Hill Foundation. I have used Hill's work on the mastermind concept personally throughout my career, for my own benefit, for work inside corporations, and as a formalized process that has birthed hundreds of professionally run groups in nearly that many different industries and professions. These days, throughout the world, there are mastermind groups of lawyers, doctors, financial advisors, Main Street merchants, service business owners, restaurant owners, etc., meeting every month, three times a year, or on some other schedule, using my format and process.

Hill discovered that Carnegie, Ford, Firestone, Edison, and others had a mastermind alliance and met regularly in order to think creatively—as they described it, their minds melding as one. They used these organized opportunities to exchange information about their discoveries and methods, share useful contacts, and find ways to create mutually profitable and intertwined business opportunities, but also to think more broadly about the economy, the world, achievement, and wealth. They told Hill that "putting their minds together" multiplied their thinking power exponentially. They and Hill alluded to a metaphysical, somewhat esoteric aspect of this you may not be willing to immediately buy into, but I can assure you from having personally organized and led these kinds of groups—with as few as four to as many as 20 participants meeting at least several times a year for two to three days at a time—that spontaneous explosions of breakthrough thought occur from the energy in the room, from the combined focus of those minds on a single problem, opportunity, or question. Whether you accept that or not, until you experience it, you can surely see the three practical, pragmatic aspects:

1. The combined experience, knowledge, and intellect far exceeds that of any individual's, therefore considerable time is rescued from duplicative trial-and-error experimentation and error, from duplicative invention and effort. Einstein said that he succeeded by groping. Every successful innovator does. But being able to benefit from the groping of a few or a dozen other smart, capable, determined individuals straightforwardly reduces the time required for each of the individuals to grope his way to the ideas and answers he needs.

2. There is also the direct exchange of useful contacts, tested and proven vendors, maybe sources of capital. Each person knows and knows of different people who, in turn, know different people, so the combined spider web of contacts is exponentially greater than any one person's.

3. Finally, there can be outright commercial, even mercenary productivity—the confidential exchange of inside information. Carnegie, Ford, Edison, Rockefeller, the bunch of them

would all be guilty of illegal insider trading by today's laws, yet to think it does not go on extensively and daily despite today's laws is foolish. Comedian Wanda Sykes says that even poor people engage in insider trading: Martha's sister-in-law who works at Wal-Mart tells her not to buy that underwear until next week 'cuz it's going on sale. Mastermind allies can pool resources and take advantage of opportunities beyond their reach as individuals. They can negotiate group discounts with vendors.

There is a "catch," however, a caution that I'll get to in a minute.

There is also a second, different application of the mastermind concept to briefly mention: its use with insiders rather than with outsiders. I have always kept a well-organized "insider's circle" around me at different times, comprised of associates, employees, critical experts, and critical vendors, who I felt I could trust to know my plans and problems and be called on to contribute their combined intelligence. There is a full description of this in Chapter 47 of my book, *No B.S. Guide to Ruthless Management of People and Profits.*

The men that Hill studied and spoke with at length about this each had his own carefully created insider's circle, his own personal mastermind alliance, typically including a treasured mentor or two, a key associate or employee, sometimes a spouse, often a "money man." Carnegie had Schwab. Rich DeVos and Jay Van Andel formed an unbreakable, lifelong mastermind alliance that built the giant Amway Corporation. Trump has had George Ross as his chief ally, advisor, and negotiator for nearly his entire real estate career, although for TV, he has a different mastermind alliance with Mark Burnett, best known for creating *Survivor*. For a time, Jobs and Wozniak. Each Disney CEO has cited a mastermind alliance with the late Walt Disney. Iacocca wrote of his "team of ten" at Chrysler. The aforementioned Ayn Rand rose to influence as a novelist turned leader of an intellectual movement with a small, tight circle of advisors and supporters.

My long-time clients Bill Guthy and Greg Renker, who developed the most successful direct-response TV company and with it a portfolio of cosmetic, skin-care, and nutrition brands, all combined generating well over $1.5 billion in yearly revenue, are both long-time, serious students of Hill and masters of the mastermind alliance approach. They are themselves a mastermind alliance of multidecade longevity. Inside their company, they join with other key individuals, like legendary infomercial producer Lenny Lieberman, in different mastermind teams for different purposes. Each brand under their corporate umbrella has its own mastermind team. Each project gets a different mastermind group brought together, and I'm pleased to say that I've been part of many of those over a very long relationship.

If you carefully look inside almost every great individual success story, you will find both the inner, inner, inner circle, and you will find that the individual was also a participant or an organizer-participant of more diverse mastermind alliances, often meeting in much the same way as the Industrial Age barons did.

The Glitch

Hill very carefully explained that a mastermind alliance required like-minded members "harmonious in thought," eager for each other's success and devoid of jealousy or envy over it, and equally eager for the success of the group as whole. That "harmonious in thought" thing is very, very tricky. This is why the mastermind alliance group system that I've developed involves four keys:

1. Organizing people with a certain commonality in type or size of business or strategic purpose.

2. A strong, knowledgeable leader sufficiently respected to wield authority over the group.
3. That leader having full or final say over selection of—or rejection of or ousting of—members of the group.
4. Fee-paid participation.

For example, at GKIC*, I currently lead the highest level mastermind group, the Titanium Mastermind, for information marketers, i.e., peers such as authors, publishers, and niche industry advisors and trainers, with at least a seven-figure yearly income from their information marketing businesses (which are often side businesses). There are a maximum of 20 in the group. They pay about $30,000.00 a year to be in the group, for my role as its leader-facilitator, and for a collection of products and services from GKIC, including the Diamond level membership. I choose who is in the group, and every year I do say no to inappropriate people. I am trusted by the members to safeguard the integrity of the group so that each person "taking" and benefiting has the capability for equivalent "giving" and contributing to others in the group and to the group as a whole.

There is another Platinum Mastermind also for information marketers, but with wider latitude in its member criteria, accommodating relative beginners and smaller-size business operators. It is led by a GKIC executive, currently Dave Dee.

There is one other GKIC group, not bound by common type of business, but by shared purpose. It is the Peak Performers/ Implementation Group, currently led by Lee Milteer. Its members are in very diverse businesses and professions, but share a passionate personal interest in the strategies, tactics, and tools of

---

*I would strongly suggest finding a mastermind group or possibly a couple that fit all the criteria I've described here to participate in. At GKIC, we can help you with that. Visit www.DanKennedy.com/mastermind.

personal performance, including goal-setting, strategic thinking, creative thinking, developing and adhering to best practices, utilizing habitforce, effectively managing change, and improving communication and persuasion skills.

All these groups meet three times per calendar year, with conference calls in between, online community and resources, and other controlled communication.

There are also local GKIC Chapters led by Certified Independent Business Advisors in many cities in the U.S. and abroad that provide several different mastermind-esque environments for entrepreneurs to meet and exchange ideas and information.

In all these cases, there is a leader at the helm, with a firm hand on the tiller, in combat with The Glitch.

I have witnessed countless ad hoc groups, with nobody paying an organizing entity to participate, no governing authority, and no designated, accepted leader in charge of everything from selection to "trains running on time." They all either fail to serve all members, disintegrate into mere congenial clubs, or collapse in acrimony. Often the person loosely organizing them has done so out of his own need to be important or for the simple mercenary purpose of creating business relationships with the invited members. Because there is no membership contract and no fee of significance paid, attendance and participation is spotty. I believe participating in such groups is a foolish waste of time. I recognize that sounds self-serving, but please understand I have no need to convince you one way or another. I frequently watch people I know delude themselves, believing such fraternal gatherings are actual mastermind alliances.

Failure

Mastermind alliances can and do fail. Some years back, I partnered with a client and assisted him with organizing a mastermind-based program for dentists, with the shared strategic purpose of marketing to and providing services to patients with a specific disease. Although the initiative had a fast and successful launch, with about 30 doctors from all over the country quickly joining the program, it subsequently fizzled and fell apart. With 20/20 hindsight, I can see many contributing factors, including our failing to be strict in selection, poorly managed expectations for the group, and others. Ultimately, simply, the requirements laid out by Napoleon Hill weren't met. Further, my #2 criteria wasn't fully met. Its leader was too nice and too accommodating, and let control of the group and its collective commitment slip away. This is not an indictment of anybody—me, my client, or the participants. It reveals that very smart, capable, successful people can screw this up! The mastermind concept drawn from Napoleon Hill's work is not at all easy to implement and sustain.

I'm pleased to say that I have very successfully organized and run five different kinds of mastermind groups, some continuing for as long as 11 years with better than a 50% stability of membership year-to-year. Recently, I ran (with an associate) a two-year program for financial advisors with sevem-figure incomes, specializing in retirement planning for boomers and seniors, a group of obviously high-income, strong-willed, experienced, and opinionated men and women. It was a grand success. My Titanium Group for information marketers is in its second year as I write this. It is basically a rebirth of a group I ran for a decade, including members who've been with me for that long.

From all this, I've learned that running these groups, participating in them fairly, and benefiting from them significantly requires, as Hill said, real commitment. I have also seen that they are well worth the committed effort. The speed of accomplishment and leaps in innovation and business growth that occur, that could only occur through this process, are often amazing although frequently a norm.

The Secret of Sunken Cost: Why We Stay in Dysfunctional Relationships

Your ability to successfully manage your time for profit has a great deal to do with the people you permit to be in your world in working relationships with you. Very often, entrepreneurs coming to grips with the realities of time presented in this book remain bound by reluctance to put at risk or sever any of these established relationships. But once you realize someone is holding you back or doing you harm, why should it be so hard to send them packing? Once you realize you are pouring time into an unsuccessful venture, project, or partnership, why is it so hard to exit and invest your time elsewhere?

Hal Arkes, a psychologist at Ohio State University, has spent much of his time studying the sunken cost phenomenon. It works like this: The more invested you are in something, intellectually, emotionally, in ego, or financially, the harder it is to stop investing more in it, long after a rational voice inside your own head has begun telling you that you are in a dead end. Arkes, quoted in a *New Yorker* article (1–21–13), explained, "Abandoning a project (practice or person) you've invested a lot in feels like you've wasted everything, and waste is something we're told to avoid." This is why people sit through a three-hour movie judged terrible an hour in—we've already paid for the ticket. It's also why companies and

The Secret of Sunken Cost, continued

their leaders stay committed to very bad business plans—we've already invested millions. Perversely, because there is so much sunken cost, people feel compelled to sink more money or time in.

It happens to otherwise smart people and organizations. One of the world's most successful restaurant companies, that I choose not to name, bought a small chain very different from its other restaurants and poured umpteen millions into it, with worsening results for years before finally dumping it for a fraction of what it paid, let alone sunk in. Cutting its losses as soon as it became clear it was a poor match with its business, and probably a poor business period, would have saved tens of millions of dollars of profit plus creative talent and time that could have been invested more productively. This is an oft-repeated story.

This is the exact opposite of Tex Bix Bender's cowboy advice: The first thing to do when you find yourself in a deep hole is—stop digging. But cutting our losses is antithetical to all we've been taught, told, and conditioned to believe about commitment and persistence and Churchill's "Never, never, never give up" and Lombardi's "Quitters never win and winners never quit." The danger of the sunken cost dilemma is that the longer we postpone loss cutting, the harder it becomes.

I have long practiced and taught what I call the Principle of the Swift Sword. I've returned substantial retainers to clients after only days or weeks, when they've misbehaved and demonstrated they are going to be "difficult." I've pronounced business projects and ad campaigns DOA after the briefest, cheapest possible tests. I tell myself and my entrepreneur clients that there is no shortage of interesting, productive,

The Secret of Sunken Cost, continued

and profitable things to apply time, talent, energy, and capital to. There's no reason to pour it down a black hole.

In a study of the NBA and the NFL, it was discovered that high draft picks and players with giant contracts invariably get more playing opportunity than lower draft picks and less costly players, regardless of whether their performance justifies it. Egos and reputations are tied to the sunken cost in these players, so better players may sit on the bench for months or even years, facts be damned. The author of *The New Yorker* article, James Surowiecki, correctly noted that this did not happen with the 2012 Seattle Seahawks. The starting quarterback, Matt Flynn, had been signed to a hefty free agent contract, much of it guaranteed, but was playing poorly in training camp, outshined by a rookie, Russell Wilson. Flynn was benched, Wilson played, and the team made it to the playoffs. This happened, Surowiecki contends, only because the decision-makers at the Seahawks disregarded sunken cost. Head coach Pete Carroll said, "I don't want contracts or salaries or investments to matter to me. You want the best guy at that time to play."

So what does all this mean to you? If you are to succeed with a dynamic new approach to managing your time for maximum gain and benefit, you must steel yourself to disregard sunken cost in your own past practices, in established relationships of all kinds, and in specific individuals you may have years and a great deal of money invested in. Now, you need relationships that work for you and people who accept, cooperate with, and support your goals.

Further, going forward, beware the sunken cost syndrome and favor the swift sword.

CHAPTER 11

Buy Time by Buying
Expertise

An expert is a man who has made all the mistakes
which can be made in a very narrow field.

—Niels Bohr, Danish Physicist

O ften, you can do something you are not knowledgeable about or skilled at yourself, and many people do
a great deal of this. But at what cost? There is time
trade-off. That time could have been invested in some highest
and best use, yielding far more in profit than the money saved
by the do-it-yourself activity you are ill-prepared for. You *can*
get everything done by whoever is most conveniently available,
who offers the cheapest price—but at what cost? Having to
micro-manage an untrustworthy provider or having to oversee
getting something attempted three times before it is done right
has a time cost and, if your time has value, is a false bargain.
Or you can seek out the best available expert, pay his price or
fee, and get the best advice or service, get the task done right

the first time, and be free of worry, stress, or battles so you can concentrate on the highest and best use of your time.

I have, for example, "my guy," Arthur Knight, who takes care of all my cars—currently four classic automobiles I drive. They are not museum pieces. His auto service business is not bargain priced, yet it is a time bargain for me. When something needs doing, my time consumption is limited to a single phone call. He or his staff person comes and gets the car, leaves a luxury car in its place, fixes whatever needs to be fixed, returns my car with gas tank full and freshly washed, takes their car, and goes. I never take a car there, never sit in a waiting room, never need to rejuggle a schedule. Over time, he sufficiently impressed me that I partnered with him in a different auto-related business that you can see at www.ImperialAutoCastle.com. It's a luxury residence for classic and exotic cars, and one of the benefits it gives its members is time. Concierge service includes delivery of the member's car anywhere in the service zone when he wishes to drive it, and pickup and return to its safe, secure home until he wishes to enjoy it again.

I have long sought access and support from the best provider I could find in any and every category as a means of buying time by buying expertise and reliability, and I have always been prepared to "overpay" in order to be their client, customer, or patient. I began this practice when it was a financial hardship, and I know it was more difficult then than when money is no longer an issue. I also know that the habit of choosing false bargains can forever prevent and prohibit you from ever getting to the level of successful accomplishment where money is no longer an issue!

In my field, where I sell my services as a marketing strategist and direct-response copywriter, there exists a wide range of fees and prices. You can find professional copywriters who will create a direct-mail campaign for a $500.00 fee, for $5,000.00, and $50,000.00 and up, and I am in that top tier of compensation.

When it's done, if it's 16 pages of sales copy, why pay $50,000.00 when you could pay $5,000.00? Size and scope of the client's opportunity matters. Whether the campaign has potential for evergreen, or long life or recurring use, or is a one-time promotion matters. But what also matters is the comparative experience and expertise of the copywriter and what translates to results, early success vs. repetitive experimentation, and performance without babysitting. I, for example, have been doing this work for 40 years, have a fine track record, and can be counted on to perform without supervision. What actually governs a client's decision is his sensitivity to the value of his time.

When you buy this kind of expertise, you don't buy deliverables by number of pages or word count, or hours, or pounds.

A Coach for Everything

It may surprise you to know that there are coaches for just about everything. There are coaches for new parents, coaches for people trying to lose weight, coaches for business. Late in his life, the great golfer Arnold Palmer found his aging body required changes to his golf swing, so he hired a coach to assist him. Highly successful people are not at all unwilling to buy coaching—in fact, they are more prone to do so, at significant fees, than are average people. There is, for example, a weight-loss coach with a practice in New York, with fees starting at $10,000.00. That's a leap up from going to Weight Watcher meetings. When Warren Buffett became seriously interested in playing cards, he reportedly retained a very successful player as his private coach. Speed to competence or to results, the compression of time required to learn something by your own efforts has high value to anyone whose time has or needs to have high value.

I have entrepreneurs as private coaching clients who pay upwards from $34,000.00 a year for a private 20-minute phone call each month and one day once a year. It is not at all uncommon for entrepreneurs to have a private coach, who acts as sounding board, confidante, advisor, creative muse, quasi-therapist, and accountability proctor. The money clients spend for this can be a grand bargain because a small amount of time given to very focused discussion with an exceptionally knowledgeable coach can sharply raise the value of all their other time.

A lot of successful businesspeople also participate in group coaching programs, where individuals with business, professional, or interest commonality come together in group meetings and in online forums, and essentially share a coach or team of coaches. At GKIC, there is a program like this called the Peak Performers/Implementation Group, led by the celebrated peak performance coach Lee Milteer and a team of other coaches. You can get information at www.DanKennedy.com/coaching and at www.milteer.com, or in due course after accepting the free offer on page 185 of this book.

The Expertise Legitimacy Test

When you are going to hire an advisor, consultant, coach, or other expert, it is important to accurately assess their actual expertise. Here are four questions to consider.

1. *Has the expert actually done the thing he is advising you about?* Or is he an academic theorist giving book reports? You can't rule the latter kind of advisor out entirely. Years ago, a client of mind used a college professor with zero practical experience to develop an employee assessment that measured honesty/dishonesty, and it proved extremely accurate and also commercially valuable. But generally speaking, if I own an NFL team, I'd like my

coach to have played the game successfully. I want my financial advisor to be a successful investor. I don't want a fat doctor who smokes. For the entrepreneur, specifically, a lot of time is wasted on self-appointed, full of B.S. experts eager to spend somebody else's money. The late, great, renowned copywriter Gary Halbert's endorsement of me was that I was one of the few copywriters who consistently had myself as a client and put my own money at risk on my own marketing projects, not just clients' money at risk in situations where I got paid, win, lose, or draw.

Not too long ago, I decided I wanted to take a serious step forward with something long of casual interest: writing mystery novels. I did not waste my time with college professors or writing coaches who have never been published or managed to get a book published a decade ago. I sought out a currently working, successful mystery writer with 25 books to his credit and arranged to be a contributing co-author to a book of his, with a backdrop I knew a lot about (harness racing), so I could learn by looking over his shoulder as he worked and pick his brain throughout the process. The resulting book, *Win, Place or Die*, hit bookstores mid-2013. Information about it can be found at the main author's website, www.LesRoberts.com.

Some years ago when I decided I wanted to invest in real estate, I did not settle just for getting information from books, courses, classes, seminars, or coaches—especially a community college professor who might own one rental house. Through my work, I met a very successful investor in commercial properties who also took on clients and investor partners. And the fact that he was in Iowa and now all my property investments are in Iowa, distant from my homes, was irrelevant.

When I got serious about estate planning, I first studied up, so I could ask intelligent questions. Then I took pains to utilize a knowledgeable intermediary, from a banking relationship, to make recommendations of not one but four potential attorneys and law firms that might suit me. Then I conducted audition interviews with all four—arranged by him, each 30 minutes, back-to-back, one right after the other, at a conference room borrowed in the bank branch 5 minutes from my house. I looked for the best expert, and I did it with good time efficiency.

2. *Is the expert current?* There are a lot of "former" and "ex" folks who hang out the expert advisor shingle after exiting the game, and soon are advising from waning memory rather than practical experience.

3. *Does the expert have satisfied clients?* Yes, I know, even Bernie Madoff had satisfied clients. But you at least want to avoid experts without satisfied clients. A good, general, time-saving, disaster-preventing litmus test that entrepreneurs should apply to anybody they are considering getting in bed with in deals or relying on for advice is: Are there at least three other successful entrepreneurs who have done more than one deal with you? Are there at least three other successful entrepreneurs who have relied on you over a lengthy period of time or repeatedly?

Show me at least three who are in love. Incredibly, I've had clients do business with people they knew full well couldn't pass this test. Greed of the moment triumphed over prudent judgment, with high costs of time and money to follow. I said: What made you think you'd be the first? This is like being the young woman, as I recall a hotel employee, who claimed she innocently accompanied Mike Tyson to his hotel room, alone, at night, and was then shocked beyond all imagination that he sexually assaulted her. Mike Tyson. And she expected a poetry reading? Some years ago, there was a guy who went deep into the forest for an entire year to observe and film bears for a documentary. He convinced himself the bears had human-like intelligence and emotions, and grew to like him. He decided to join them in their cave. Where they ate him. I found this hilarious. In short, a bear is a bear that will do what bears do.

4. *Do you understand what your chosen expert is doing and how he does it?* That gets us back to Bernie and how he made off with all that money from all those people who should have known better and were more victims of their own greed and willful blindness than of him. Never blindly delegate to mystics. If you can't understand how the investment makes money, how the sales strategy works, how the expert's advice about anything works—run.

My best clients are very smart about marketing—not naïve or uninformed. My best copywriting clients are actually capable of writing pretty good copy themselves, but have higher and better uses of their time and recognize superior, specialized expertise on my part. They understand what I'm doing even if they can't do it as well, so they can fairly judge and can offer legitimate critical questions.

Invest to Move Up and Speed Up

The assistance of the right expert can produce a quantum leap up and a dramatic acceleration in speed of achievement. Frequently, my clients have to "stretch," financially and mentally, to sign on with me, but then save enormous amounts of time otherwise taken by trial and error experimentation, having to search for important contacts or vendors, and enduring a difficult learning curve. A good example is a client, a chiropractor, Dr.

Chris Tomshack, who decided in 2006 he wanted to take the successful model of his four clinics and franchise it to clinics nationwide. This big step up was accomplished with record-breaking speed, hitting 20-plus operating units in the first few months, now pushing 400 franchised clinics nationwide. He was able to step up to a much higher level of business, from small business owner to CEO of a nationwide company with multi-million dollar revenues, and do so at breakneck speed safely and successfully in part thanks to my expert coaching, and in part to other connections I assisted him in making. These two aspects of success—moving up and speeding up—are almost always better accomplished with smart investment in other people's experience and expertise instead of just investing directly in business development.

Interesting Experts

The Time-Saving Approach to Romance

Krista White is a professional matchmaker, and the President of the famous It's Just Lunch matchmaking franchise, in the Washington, DC, Fairfax County, Virginia, and Montgomery County, Maryland, areas. It often surprises people that the majority of her clients cover a wide age range, from 40 to late 60s, but share in common being busy professionals, executives, and entrepreneurs with significant success and high incomes and net worth, who are all perfectly capable of getting their own dates—but come to realize they cannot *efficiently* get the right dates.

Both accomplished men and women sign on as clients, to be coached, professionally represented to carefully selected individuals,

Interesting Experts, continued

and have their first dates arranged for them, all for a fee. Many have tired of the randomness and futile time consumption of fix-ups by family or friends, online dating, and bar scene or social function pickups, and many are engaged in business or professional lives that make openly searching for dates via online sites or in social settings unsafe or potentially embarrassing.

The idea that only "losers who can't find a date" retain matchmakers like Krista and her expert team is quickly dispelled by a look at the profiles of her clients, which I was given a look at, confidentially, when doing some consulting work for her business. (One of the unique factors of her service is that no client's profile or information is made public or placed in accessible forums. Matches are individually arranged.) They work with over 1,000 clients at any given time, those who have made the decision that time can be saved even in romance by hiring expert assistance. You can see Krista's business at www.KristaWhiteMatchmaker.com.

From Zero to Successful Published Author in 90 Days

Adam Witty has put in one place, under one roof, an incredible team of experts and a portfolio of services that can take just about anyone to having a well-written, high quality book written, published, and promoted in 90 days or less. For many professionals and entrepreneurs, being the author of a published book provides strong competitive advantage and authority, status, and trust benefits. Having a book trumps all other marketing media. But most entrepreneurs will instantly disqualify themselves with "I can't write" or "I certainly can't write a whole book—I wouldn't even know where to begin" or "I don't have the time—it will take forever!"

Interesting Experts, *continued*

Adam's Advantage Publishing Group offers a one- to two-day "Talk Your Book" speed service. The client camps at their offices for a day or, at max, two, is interviewed by experts for his book, audio and video recorded for promotional media, photographed, and the book's website laid out. Then the client leaves, and Adam's ghostwriters, editors, graphic designers, web team, and publicists take over. The author's subsequent time consumption is minor, mostly given to approvals of work done. In three months or sooner, he has a terrific published book in his hands, in national distribution including Amazon, supported with its own website. The time saved by this expert assembly line is inestimable. You can learn more at http://AdvantageFamily.com.

Famous, Fast

Many entrepreneurs, executives, and professionals, and/or their companies, can profit from fame; from media exposure; and, mostly, the ability to reference that media exposure in all their own advertising and marketing. For different people, the "as seen on" credit—CNN, FOX, PBS, etc., and the "as seen in" credit—*Forbes, USA Today, People,* etc.—has great influence and value. Achieving it via do-it-yourself contact with media outlets and producers, editors, and journalists can consume huge amounts of time and be a momentous struggle. Hiring a traditional publicist can consume months and large sums, and still offer an unreliable result.

Nick Nanton and Jack Dicks have created a radically different, high-speed approach to creating this same exposure and media credits for the clients of their Celebrity Branding Agency, with

Interesting Experts, continued

absolute certainty. I won't spill the beans here, but their clients—
doctors, lawyers, financial advisors, professional speakers, business owners of every stripe—gain the halo of national fame and
expert status with media credits, starting from zero, in a matter
of months. Nick Nanton is also an Emmy-winning documentary
filmmaker, who creates powerful promotional documentaries
for clients, and even arranges to have them aired on PBS, FOX,
and History Channel affiliates, getting that "as seen on" credit.
You can learn about their speed to celebrity system at www.
CelebrityBrandingAgency.com.

There Are No Do-Overs

Ron and Jill Wolforth run the nation's most successful coaching program for junior high school, high school, and college-age
baseball players showing exceptional promise and for the parents
of these players. Whether they are high school players interested
in college scholarships and making it onto top college rosters or
players who hope and display the potential to become professionals and get to The Big Show, Ron provides one-to-one and
group coaching, including work at their Texas baseball ranch,
online and tele-coaching, analysis of video of players, and much
more. Ron and Jill also coach the parents on every aspect of managing their son's development, from injury prevention to college
career to pro career.

Ron is the author of the leading book in this subject cat-
egory, *A Parent's Survival Guide: For the Parent of the Elite
Pitcher,* and you can see more about their unusual business at
PitchingCentral.com. Ron points out that a young athlete of

Interesting Experts, continued

promise only gets one opportunity; no one can command another supply of time and a do-over of the years leading up to success at the collegiate or pro level.

• • • • •

The clients of these expert advisors, consultants, and coaches are all, in various ways, buying time by buying expertise. It's often true that the most expensive time is that consumed by unnecessary trial-and-error experimentation and re-inventing wheels. Smart, highly successful people never see obtaining expert assistance as a sign of weakness, but as an intelligent means of buying time, efficiency, speed, and greater certainty of desired outcomes.

CHAPTER 12

The Inner Game of Peak
Personal Productivity

My mother said to me, "If you become a soldier you'll be a general;
if you become a monk, you'll end up as the Pope." Instead,
I became a painter and wound up as Picasso.

—PABLO PICASSO

Y ou can load yourself up with big, hunky day
planner devices, computer software, notepads, different
colored pens, stickers, strings tied around your thumbs,
and a million little "techniques," and you'll still be pitifully
unproductive if you don't have your "inner game" under
control. Productivity is an inside-out game.

Psycho-Cybernetics and Getting More
Value from Your Time

You probably recognize the term "Psycho-Cybernetics." The
book of that title has sold more than 30 million copies worldwide.
Several different audio program adaptations have been sold via

the famous Nightingale-Conant catalog, the SkyMall catalog, a TV program, and bookstores. The mental training techniques created by Dr. Maxwell Maltz that make up Psycho-Cybernetics have been endorsed and used by famous pro athletes and coaches, leading corporate executives, star salespeople, entertainment personalities, and by me. Salvador Dali gave Dr. Maltz an original painting as thanks for Psycho-Cybernetics' influence on his career.

When Dr. Maltz first began putting his techniques down on paper in the 1960s, he was far ahead of his time, so far ahead that people first discovering his material right now are amazed by and profit enormously from them.

What does all that have to do with you and peak productivity?

There is a certain state of mind that best facilitates achieving peak productivity. You can best create that state of mind as needed, when needed, at will, by mastering certain Psycho-Cybernetics techniques.

For example, Dr. Maltz talked about "clearing the calculator." If you have a simple calculator laying around, get it, and take a look at it. You'll find that you have to hit the "clear" button and either store in memory or completely clear away one problem before you employ the calculator to solve another. In his studies of human behavior, Dr. Maltz observed that all too often we're trying to use our minds to work on several problems at once, without ever stopping to hit the "clear" button.

Achieving maximum personal productivity requires that you become extraordinarily facile at stopping, storing, and clearing so as to direct 100% of your mental powers to one matter at a time, to the matter at hand. One client of mine, the CEO of a $20 million-a-year corporation, is a compulsive, obsessive worrier. He admittedly lets a dozen worries loose to run around in his mind at the same time while he is trying to do something else and says he is constantly interrupted by his own thoughts. He marvels at me and tells others that "it is amazing how Kennedy can just box up a problem, put it away on a shelf in his mind, focus totally on some task, and only go back to work on the problem when he wants to." This is because I have practiced and practiced and practiced the technique of "clearing the calculator" until it is second nature to me.

A big reason for my prolific output as a writer is that I never have to "get in the mood" to write. Many people go through great physical and mental gyrations just getting ready to get ready to write. I don't. I can sit down, put my fingers on the keys, clear my calculator in 60 seconds or less, and write.

This is just one of a number of simple but very powerful Psycho-Cybernetic techniques, but it illustrates a very important point: *if you can't control your thoughts and manage your mind, you can't control or manage your time.*

Creating a Peak Productivity Environment

You can do a number of things to make certain that your environment works *for* you instead of against you. The following are some key ideas to consider and experiment with.

- Psychological triggers
- Organization vs. clutter

As I said, I am a big believer in populating my work environment with "psychological triggers"—objects that remind me to think a certain way. I work at mentally attracting wealth, for example, so my primary work environment is full of things that represent wealth: at last count 27 such pictures, objects, and artifacts were within view. Because I am very concerned with time, I have eight clocks around me. I have a wooden hangman's noose to remind me of deadlines. A painting on my wall of a black tiger devouring a man in the jungle reminds me of the quote "Tigers starve last in the jungle," and reminds me to be tough and aggressive.

I think you can "surround yourself" three possible ways:

1. By accident and happenstance, with no purpose in mind and no purpose served.
2. Consciously or unconsciously, with things that trigger negative responses: frustration, anger, resentment, depression.
3. Deliberately with things selected to reinforce positive—productive—responses.

"A Clean Desk Is a Sign of a Sick Mind"

Let's not be dogmatic about this. I suspect that a person with a constantly, pristinely clean and neat desk and work environment—a "Felix"—may very well be neurotic. Certainly I *prefer* to believe that. On the other hand, the person immersed in clutter and a chaotic environment—an "Oscar"—MUST waste time by hunting and searching, must be distracted. There is a broad band of acceptable style between the two extremes.

Personally, fortunately, largely by "clearing the calculator," I can sit down and work effectively surrounded by clutter or in chaos. However, I will tell you that I am most productive in what I have come to call a "semi-organized environment." As a writer, for example, I think having stacks of papers, reference materials, and other documents around is unavoidable, but I find it very helpful to have those piles organized by topic or project.

Really creative, innovative thinking seems to come out of chaos more often than out of neatnik organization. But the successful implementation

> One big time-saving tip I can give you is: When in doubt, throw it out.

of innovative ideas seems to come about in a most organized, disciplined way.

It's worth noting, to paraphrase management guru Peter Drucker, that what we are after is *effectiveness,* not necessarily *efficiency.* Put a time-and-motion analyst on the typical entrepreneur, and he will come up empty. How do you analyze the guy who sits on the floor of his office watching daytime TV talk shows and thumbing through magazines for hours on end, then suddenly hits upon the right "pitch" for his company's new fitness product?

The most important thing here is to be honest with yourself. Is the level of clutter and disorganization around you helping or hindering? Out of control or just about right?

Many people are compulsive keepers. I find a bit of ruthlessness toward paper is beneficial. If you seriously doubt you will need or use it again, go ahead and throw it out immediately. If it becomes really important, it will be provided to you again. At least once a year, usually in December, I conduct a violent purge of my correspondence files, client records, desk drawers, etc., and throw out as much of it as I

N ot too long ago, I moved much of my home office, files, records, and library from one home to another. More than 100 boxes. Because I'm busy, some of those boxes have yet to be opened years later, and that's because no need has sent me into them, looking for anything. Undoubtedly, by the time I get around to opening them, I'll be able to throw out what's in them. Which probably means it didn't need to be kept in the first place. I'm making a note to myself: Be even MORE ruthless.

dare. In all these years, I've had that come back to haunt me only a couple of times.

It's also important for your "workspace" to make it easy for you to work. My own, in my home office, is not unlike a pilot's cockpit; without getting out of my swivel chair, I can operate my computers, my TV, and my CD player. I can reach my most important reference books, and I have two "surfaces" for paperwork. Once you get to work, you ought to be able to stay at work without having to jump up and down every minute or two to fetch something or put something else away.

Finally—The Militant Attitude

I have come to really, deeply, vehemently, violently *resent* having my time wasted. I place a very, very high value on my time, and I believe that the value you really, honestly place on your time will control the way others value it and you.

I have talked about this elsewhere in this book and do not want to redundantly beat up on any one single point, yet this self-determination is so important. You set your own price. And you determine whether or not people "get it" and respect it.

When I was in direct sales, managing, motivating, and trying to help others build their businesses, I was constantly amazed and often depressed at how little value people placed on their time and how pitifully unwilling they were to protect it and wisely invest it. I heard "I didn't because . . . my mother-in-law decided to surprise us with a visit . . . my buddy Bob dropped by and took up the whole evening . . . the roof started to leak, and I had to work on that . . ." And on and on. But if you already had something very important to do, that you were committed to doing, mother-in-law would have to sit home alone and watch TV, buddy Bob would be bounced out, a bucket would be put under the leak, and you'd stay focused.

How tough are you on those who would undervalue your time? How tough are you on yourself?

The Unreasonable Man

I needed to find and choose an estate planning attorney. What most people in my place would wind up doing is going to several different attorneys' offices on different days to meet with each one. Drive here, there. Find a place to park. Wait in their waiting rooms. I had my private banker choose three for me to interview and get them booked for 30-minute appointments, back-to-back, in a borrowed office at my bank branch 5 minutes from my house. The attorneys made 30- and 40-minute drives—not me. Attorney #2 waited in a waiting room. I did not wait. My time was used very efficiently while, candidly, theirs was not.

Were I on the other side of this, a lawyer asked to audition in this manner, inconveniencing myself with no fee and no reasonable certainty of securing a client, having to drive to a meeting place and be one of three auditioning, I would, of course, refuse. Not only is it poor time management, it's poor positioning. There is a marketing answer to such a request— refer to the books *No B.S. Sales Success in The New Economy* and *No B.S. Guide to Trust-Based Marketing*. But the fact that I would never agree to this were I a lawyer has no bearing whatsoever on my willingness to demand it of these lawyers. Please re-read that sentence; then think of it in broader context. Neither the reasonableness of your demands or rules implemented to maximize the value of your time or how you would feel about them if somebody were trying to impose them on you matters. Not a whit. If you are to optimize your time, you are going to be unreasonable by others' and by ordinary standards.

The golden rule must be suspended. If you will only do unto others as you would have them do unto you, you're screwed—

because few others properly value or manage their time. If you are succeeding properly as an entrepreneur, your time must be worth considerably more than virtually everybody else's. The lawyers I met with bill their hours at $200.00 to $300.00. I bill mine at $2,000.00, and no work hour can be worth less than $2,000.00 for me to hit my income targets. (See Chapter 1.) This isn't about morality and moral equivalency. It's about *math*.

For me to drive 20 minutes to a lawyer's office, take 10 minutes to park and walk and go up in the elevator, reverse it to get back to my workspace, I am in the hole no less than $2,000.00. For him to come to me, he's in the hole no more than $300.00.

This is a radical idea: pragmatism.

"You May Be Able to Get Away with These Things, But I Certainly Can't—At Least Not Now"

Let's be clear about what is not required to succeed at being an Unreasonable Man. Permission is not. You dictate and impose. You do not ask. Length of time in a job, business, place is not. This power is not conferred by the passing of time. Money, success, or wealth is not. It's helpful, but it's not required. I have long had clients far wealthier than I inconvenience themselves to travel to meet with me, waiting for weeks for an opportunity to speak with me by phone, and otherwise submitting to my rules of engagement, and this predated my not caring whether someone became a client or not. In fact, doing this when you think you can't afford it is the fastest way to getting your compensation sky-high so you can afford it.

Instead, there are just three requisites, and they are all within your reach right now or at any time, because you manufacture them. You get this gold by spinning thin air.

1. Unassailable Authority
2. Celebrity

3. Deal Flow/Supply vs. Demand

By the way, should you wish to be an Equally Unreasonable Woman, I'm afraid I have bad news: You *are* at gender disadvantage. That means you must have the requisite assets times the power of three. Your Unassailable Authority must be clearer, stronger, more unassailable than a male in a comparable business, profession, or position.

Your Rules

According to the actor Michael Caine, as stated in his autobiography, *The Elephant to Hollywood,* Frank Sinatra had a 20-minute rule. If he was invited to dinner, party, or meeting and he was in his car for more than 20 minutes, he would tell his driver to turn around and take him home.

You need preset rules.

Discipline doesn't get made up as you go along.

Like Sinatra, I too have a 20-minute rule. Mine is about the phone. Fully 90% of my phone appointments with clients, would-be clients, and people doing work for me are booked in 20-minute increments. It's my experience 20 minutes is enough— if both parties are properly prepared for the call. If not, no call should occur. This allows me to fit three calls per hour. With few breaks—because I'm a camel—in a 7:00 A.M. to 7:00 P.M. "Phone Day," I can dispense with 30 phone appointments in only one day a month, and keep nearly all the other days phone free. Stop and think for a minute how the productivity of your days might change if many or most were free of any phone conversations, and you locked your phone away in a desk drawer.

Also like Sinatra, I'm not big on the inconvenience and time suck of distance. When clients come to me, they are required to stay at a very modest hotel that is less than 15 minutes from my house. Most of my everyday life is arranged within 8-minute and 15-minute to 30-minute radiuses around my house—the racetrack where most of my horses are and I drive professionally, a favorite restaurant, two additional, satisfactory restaurants, the copy shop and the package shipping and receiving store I use, a movie theater, the supermarket, and the aforementioned hotel in the 8- to 15-minute radius. The shopping area with a large Barnes & Noble store in one direction, the upscale mall in the other, a business I'm a partner in, Imperial Auto Castle, where the classic cars I drive are housed, the airport I fly in and out of, etc., in the 15- to 30-minute radius. The distance between home and racetrack was the chief element in selecting the home, but all things were considered because 90% of the time, I do not want to drive more than 15 minutes in each direction for anything or anybody. This was achieved without living in an elbow-to-elbow dense, traffic-gridlocked city. Actually, this is in a semi-rural small town.

My specifics need not be your specifics—that's not my point. But you should want to and can consciously, deliberately, strategically choose and control where you live and work, what you will and will not do, and how others are permitted to consume your time. **You really have to get that it is all *your* time. *All* of it. *Every* minute of it. *Yours*.** If I let a client stay at a hotel 30 minutes away instead of 8, I have let him take 22 minutes x 2, 44 minutes of *my* time that I could have kept for myself. Didn't I have something to do with it? When you permit people to take 30 minutes for a business phone conversation that could have been accomplished in 20, you let them take—and waste—10 minutes of *your* time. Let that happen twice a day, 250 work days a year, it's 5,000 minutes. In 5 years, 25,000 minutes. 416 hours. 52 eight-hour days. In a 40-year career, 200,000 minutes. 3,334 hours. 416 days. Now, what is it you said you don't have the time to do?—read and study? Write a good newsletter for your customers every month? Exercise? Take a decent vacation?

My rules—or Sinatra's—need not be your rules. The point is, you should have rules. Without rules, you have anarchy. That anarchy equals freedom is an epic lie. It destroys it. The absence of curfews of any kind does not constitute the absolute freedom to stroll about the streets at any time you please—if those streets are unsafe and you risk mugging or violent assault at any time. The absence of winter street parking bans so that everyone has absolute freedom to park as they please on both sides of the street gives no one true freedom if the snow plows can't clear the street and no one can go anywhere for weeks. These sorts of rules imposed by others chafe but are pretty much necessary to prevent a *Lord of the Flies* scenario. But, the rules you make and impose on yourself and others need not chafe you. You craft them to your benefit. You use them to organize your life and the world around you to safeguard your time, energy, productivity, and peace of mind. This is even a constitutional right in the United States—"pursuit of happiness."

There's an old, little book I've had for decades in my library, with a beautiful title: *The Kingship of Self-Control.* Its title alone is a course. Kingship. Yes, you can be king of all you survey. You get kingship by controlling yourself, and by your exercising control over others. Conversely, you get peonage and enslavement by failing to exercise control over yourself and others. Do you want to live as king or peon? A king is a ruler. By definition, a ruler makes and enforces rules. Only by adopting the behavior of a king do you get to be a king.

The Inner Game of Kingship

You need not impose control in a mean-spirited or diva-like manner.

There's no need to be mean. You can be polite yet firm. You can present your rules of engagement as beneficial to those you work with as well as to yourself. You can good-humoredly acknowledge eccentricity on your part. You can *sell* your way of doing things. (I didn't say: negotiate. I said: sell.)

There's no need to be a diva about it. This isn't about demanding only blue M&Ms and Hawaiian water in your dressing room. This isn't about egotism at all. Your decisions about how and when the world interacts with you are pragmatic, albeit personal. They should be reasoned, not arbitrary.

For these reasons, you must not let yourself be made to feel guilty. There's nothing in this to be guilty about. The bus driver never feels guilty about not pulling up to any bus stop in the city the instant you arrive there—he makes his appointed rounds on a set schedule. If that inconveniences you, there are other transportation choices available. I think of the way I work in much the same way. There are other choices. If someone is or feels unbearably inconvenienced by the way I make my appointed rounds on a schedule set by me, they are free to get the services I provide from another source. They are free to reject me as customer and sell to someone else. I hold no monopoly.

In my Renegade Millionaire Training, I make the point that there is never any need to be or behave like a prick in order to be successful, but you must be okay with some, possibly many people thinking of you as an insufferable prick. If you're too thin-skinned for that, extraordinary success and autonomy as an entrepreneur are well beyond your reach.

Guilt is a very powerful emotion. Most people are routinely and easily manipulated with it. Criticism, another. Most people cannot hold up to others making fun of them, being critical of them, thinking them odd. Outright dislike, another. Most people try to be liked by all and likeable to all. Most are very needy of others' approval. The entrepreneur must raise himself above these ordinary concerns. An entrepreneur seeks income and financial rewards, independence and autonomy, and other outcomes that

NO B.S. Time Management for Entrepreneurs 🌐 165

are profoundly different, apart from, and superior to those ever achieved or experienced by 95% of the people around him. That requires him to think in profoundly different and superior ways. He can't have one without the other. Success is a conceit. If he is to have it, it will be at an intellectual, emotional, and behavioral distance from most others.

The very idea of "time management" is itself a grand conceit. It says that you—*and just who do you think you are, anyway?*—are going to manage, i.e., impose control over, dictate to, and govern God's minutes and their movement, clock and calendar, people of all sorts around you. It announces that you will have your way with time. This is not a humble idea.

In the great film starring Michael Caine and Sean Connery *The Man Who Would Be King,* directed by John Huston, Caine's character, in reacting to a grandiose challenge, says, "We are not *little* people." This is what has to be decided by the entrepreneur who sets out to control his time.

Most time management training, books, courses, and lecturers focus almost entirely on mechanical methods and on tools. A better appointment book, a better software program, colored stickers, one kind of list or another. But these are no better than owning guns: They are useless without *the will* to use them.

Reasons Why a Year Passes and No Meaningful Progress Is Made

The only thing some people do is grow older.

—EDGAR HOWE, AMERICAN JOURNALIST

I wonder how many times I've heard a variation of "I've got 30 years' experience—I *should* be doing better," or "I work very hard—I *should* be doing better," or "I've got my Ph.D.—I *should* be doing better," or "I've got the best product—I *should* be doing better."

In the speaking business, I know many people believe they are much better speakers than I am. Some of them are right, and they are befuddled and antagonized by how well I've done, mystified at how I came to be on the giant public events with huge audiences and they didn't. "I'm better." "I've been at this longer." *"I should be up there instead of him."*

I suppose the biggest problem with all that is the word "should." It implies "entitlement." And our entire nation is being rotted out by the viral spread of "entitlement thinking."

Everybody seems to think they are somehow entitled to something. The Indians think they are entitled to become tax-exempt multimillionaires through gambling because of wrongs done to their ancestors. Minorities believe they are entitled to college admission and jobs based on quotas, regardless of their qualifications. Women believe they are entitled to all sorts of special treatment from employers so they can have children, raise a family, and develop a career—"have their cake and eat it too." Senior citizens believe they are entitled to government benefits far in excess of whatever they paid in, to free medical care for life, regardless of how long they live or who has to pay. We even have a nutcase congressman who has suggested that every American is entitled to a home and a job, and that our government should guarantee them these things. The so-called "Millennials" seem to think they are entitled to everything, right now, for doing nothing. And I could keep going. (Have I offended everybody yet?)

Here's the real deal: Nobody's entitled to anything but opportunity. Not even to a level playing field. Nothing. Nada. Just opportunity.

This is one reason why a person fails to advance much from one year to the next: He is so busy whining about how unfair everything is and feeling sorry for himself that he has no time left to make anything happen.

But, as Eric Hoffer, author of *The True Believer: Thoughts on the Nature of Mass Movements*, wrote:

There are many who find a good alibi far more attractive than an achievement, for an achievement does not settle anything permanently. We still have to prove that we are as good today as we were yesterday. But when we have a valid alibi for not achieving anything, we are fixed, so to speak, for life. Moreover, when we have an alibi for not writing a book and not painting a picture and so on, we have an alibi for not writing the greatest book and not painting the greatest picture. Small wonder that the effort expended and the punishment endured in obtaining a good alibi often exceed the effort and grief requisite for the attainment of a most marked achievement.

Hoffer's observation is one of the finest, most accurate, and profound I have ever encountered.

> I say: No one who is good at making excuses is also good at making money. The skills are mutually exclusive.

Alibi-itis. "I'd do that IF . . ." The kids were grown. I wasn't so tired after a day's work. I had more support from my spouse. I had a better education. I didn't live in this terrible neighborhood. And on and on and on.

How about writing a book? Scott Turow, now one of the wealthiest and most successful fiction authors of our time, wrote his first novel longhand, a page at a time, while riding the train, commuting to and from the offices of his law practice. My friends Mark Victor Hansen and Jack Canfield wrote and had published or self-published God knows how many books, audiocassettes, and entire courses with the world barely noticing. They received rejection notes from ALL the major publishers for their "ultimate brainchild" before convincing a small publisher to put out

Chicken Soup for the Soul, which has since become a juggernaut, an empire, with hundreds of titles and millions of copies sold. How about breaking into acting? Sylvester Stallone kept his belongings in a bus station locker, slept in alleys, and scrounged food from dumpsters early in his career.

So, reason number one: alibi-itis. Choosing a nifty alibi over a difficult path to achievement. That's why somebody looks around after another year has passed and is still in exactly the same place.

Majoring in Minor Matters

It never ceases to amaze me how people can manage to focus their time, energy, and resources on everything but the few vital things in their business that really have to do with directly making money.

Just recently, a fellow heard me speak at a seminar, rushed to the back of the room and bought my *"Magnetic Marketing System,"* came back to me and enthusiastically told me how much he learned from my talk and how excited he was about implementing my ideas, pumped my hand like Jack LaLanne, and tore out of there like the Tasmanian devil. About a week later, his copy of my System came into my office with the mailman, with a note sheepishly asking for a refund. On arriving home, the man discovered he already had my System, sitting on a shelf, still shrink-wrapped in plastic, purchased at a seminar over a year earlier. Now, it's not the fact that it was my System, but what on earth had he been doing every hour of every day for a year that was more important than enhancing his business's ability to attract and acquire new customers?

Not long ago, I did a bit of consulting for a guy with a small chain of retail stores. He just about begged for my help. Said he wasn't making it and had no money to do any advertising or marketing. I gave him a simple, easy-to-implement idea—a change in the way incoming calls were handled—that would easily double his sales. I know it would. It's proven. After a few months passed, I asked him how that strategy was working. He explained that he'd been too busy to try it. *Too busy doing what?* He couldn't tell me. Just too busy.

Well, here's how to get focused, if you're having trouble in that department: Identify and write down the three most important, most significant, most productive, most valuable things you can do to foster success in your particular enterprise. Just three. Write them down. From there, translate them into three actions you can take each and every day. Write them down.

For example, one of the most important things to me is a continuous stream of new requests for my services. As long as this demand for "me" exceeds the available supply of "me," I can demand and get premium fees, choose clients I like and blow off those I don't, choose projects that interest me and reject those that don't, confidently turn away business knowing the temporary vacuum will fill, and generally do as I darned well please. But if I let the demand diminish so that supply exceeds demand, I have to start compromising all over the place. So this is very important to me. What can I do every day to be certain this demand-supply ratio stays weighted in my favor?

I do not let a day go by that I do not send out a letter or a package, make or return a phone call, get an article published, do something to keep my books on bookstore shelves, secure a high-profile speaking engagement, or do something else to create and stimulate "deal flow." It doesn't matter how busy I am. Or how tired I am. Or if it's the Friday before a holiday weekend. Whatever. Before sunset, at least ONE thing will be done intended to stimulate demand.

172 ⊛ NO B.S. Time Management for Entrepreneurs

Nothing and no one can steal the time required to make certain that happens. Every single day. No exceptions. No excuses.

As a direct result, "demand" for me has steadily grown, even as the "supply" I am willing to offer has diminished, which has allowed me to very substantially raise my fees, keep raising them every year, fire troublesome clients without remorse, and do business entirely on my terms to suit me. This one single, simple discipline has been worth millions.

But I'll bet if you followed the typical entrepreneur around with a list of his "Big Three," you'd log lots of days where he "never got around to" doing any one of these three things at all. See, those days are failure days. Too many of those days guarantee he'll wind up on New Year's Day just about where he was 365 days before.

Breaking the Code of Extraordinarily Successful People

Early in my career, I was very fortunate to be exposed to some of the greatest "success educators," such as Earl Nightingale, Dr. Maxwell Maltz, Napoleon Hill, and the more contemporary Zig Ziglar and Jim Rohn. Even more recently, for ten years, I got to appear frequently as a speaker on programs with Rohn, Zig, Brian Tracy, Tom Hopkins, and others like them.

There's a point Jim made that stuck with me when I first heard him say it, when I was a kid, and that still has impact even today. It breaks the code of the highly successful person. It takes all the mystery and mystique away. When you very closely examine the highly successful person, in any field, you walk away saying to yourself:

Well, it's no wonder he's doing so well. Look at
everything he does.

CHAPTER 13 / REASONS WHY A YEAR PASSES AND NO MEANINGFUL PROGRESS IS MADE

You see, success isn't much of a mystery. In that respect, it's actually disappointing to a lot of people who want it to be very complicated, who, as we discussed earlier, prefer a good alibi. But it's just a reflection of what you are doing with your time.

I would now add to Rohn's statement, ". . . and look very closely at the one thing or two or three things he gets done without fail, every single day."

I can do a good job of predicting what your bank balance will be a year from now, if you'll give me the following information:

- What's in the account today
- A list of the books you read and audio programs you listened to last month
- Some information about the five people you hang out with most
- A little analysis of how you spend your time during an average week

For 90% of all people, by the way, making this prediction is a no-brainer. The correct guess is: same as it was last year.

If you happen to be "stuck," then just taking some action to change isn't even enough. Jim Rohn called this *"The principle of massive action."* And when you look at highly successful people, you'll find they are massive action takers. They don't just try one solution to a problem, they implement 20 all at the same time.

I once had a dentist call me, after having gone home from my weekend seminar, and tell me: "I've made a list of 300 things to change in the practice." Every week, he did ten of them. After 30 weeks, he had done everything on that list, big and small. And, without a penny increase in advertising, without a dollar's difference in marketing, in the same office, with (almost) the same staff, his practice had more than quadrupled in volume. He took massive action. When I tell the story, the usual, predictable reaction is astonishment and dismay—"*300* changes? I'd never get 300 things done."

Hopefully, armed with the information and strategies in this book, your answer will now be different.

Dan Kennedy's No B.S. Time Truths

Dan Kennedy's #1 No B.S. Time Truth
If you don't know what your time is worth, you can't expect the world to know it either.

• • • • •

Dan Kennedy's #2 No B.S. Time Truth
Time Vampires will suck as much blood out of you as you permit. If you're drained dry at day's end, it's your fault.

• • • • •

Dan Kennedy's #3 No B.S. Time Truth
If they can't find you, they can't interrupt you.

• • • • •

Dan Kennedy's #4 No B.S. Time Truth
Punctuality provides personal power.

• • • • •

Dan Kennedy's #5 No B.S. Time Truth
By all means, judge. But know that you too will be judged.

• • • • •

Dan Kennedy's #6 No B.S. Time Truth
Self-discipline is MAGNETIC.

• • • • •

Dan Kennedy's #7 No B.S. Time Truth
If you don't MANAGE information, you can't profit from information.

• • • • •

Dan Kennedy's #8 No B.S. Time Truth
Good enough is good enough.

• • • • •

Dan Kennedy's #9 No B.S. Time Truth
Liberation is the ultimate entrepreneurial achievement.

• • • • •

Other Books by the Author in the No B.S. Series, Published by Entrepreneur Press

No B.S. DIRECT Marketing for NON-Direct Marketing Businesses

No B.S. Guide to Marketing to Leading-Edge Boomers and Seniors (with Chip Kessler)

No B.S. Guide to Trust-Based Marketing (with Matt Zagula)

No B.S. Price Strategy (with Jason Marrs)

No B.S. Guide to Marketing to the Affluent

No B.S. Business Success in the New Economy

No B.S. Sales Success in the New Economy

No B.S. Wealth Attraction in the New Economy

No B.S. Guide to Ruthless Management of People and Profits

Other Books by Dan Kennedy

Ultimate Marketing Plan (4th Edition—20th Anniversary Edition), Adams Media

Ultimate Sales Letter (4th Edition—20th Anniversary Edition), Adams Media

The New Psycho-Cybernetics with Dr. Maxwell Maltz (Prentice-Hall)

Unfinished Business/Autobiographical Essays, Advantage

Making Them Believe: The 21 Principles and Lost Secrets of Dr. Brinkley-Style Marketing with Chip Kessler, GKIC/Morgan-James

Make 'Em Laugh & Take Their Money, GKIC/Morgan-James

Other Books

Uncensored Sales Strategies by Sydney Barrows (with Dan Kennedy), Entrepreneur Press

Index

THE MOST INCREDIBLE
Free Gift EVER

*Learn How to claim your $633.91 Worth of Pure,
Powerful Money-Making Information Absolutely FREE*

*Including a FREE "Test-Drive" of
GKIC Insider's Circle Gold Membership*

All You Have To Do is Go Here Now:
www.DanKennedy.com/time

6